CREAM CITY HUSTLE

James C. Molet

JAMES C. MOLET

Published by JCM Publishing, Sierra Vista, AZ 85635.

ISBN: 978-0-9895505-4-3

Cream City Hustle

For permission to use all other material within this book please contact the author, James C. Molet: jcm.publishing@yahoo.com
Subscribe to http://RetirementSavvy.net, where personal finance, with a focus on retirement planning, is covered via Discussions, Recommendations, Interviews, Quizzes and the Living Frugally series.

CONTENTS

ACKNOWLEDGEMENTS

Sincere gratitude and thanks are extended to the following that helped to bring my first novel into being:

My wife, Karen, my daily sounding board and the partner that makes most of my successes possible.

My brother, Kem, a fan of fictional thrillers, for his early reviews and the encouragement to continue writing the story.

The book's Editor, Brian D. Tramuel, for catching all the typographical errors I missed and his attention to the rhythm of the story. His contributions were invaluable.

Thank you all.

PROLOGUE

Near West Side. Chicago. To the casual observer, not much ever happened near the intersection of South Keeler Avenue and West Roosevelt Road. An abandoned warehouse fills one corner, stretching half a block in either direction. Empty lots littered with trash and empty bottles, long ago abandoned by would be entrepreneurs, occupy two corners opposite one another. The last corner is home to a run-down strip mall populated by a hair salon, a barber shop, a Bar-B-Q joint and a storefront church where the Southern style gospel music that escapes through the entrance is the only source of inspiration in an otherwise grim reality. Near West Side, Chicago is not a Norman Rockwell image of America.

On this sleepy Thursday afternoon however, something did happen. Anyone who had stumbled into the warehouse and back into the room that formerly housed the Human Resources department, would have been witness to justice, as administered on the cold, hard streets of Chicago. He never would have imagined, at 27 years of age, that he would pee himself. But that was exactly what had happened. After binding his hands and feet, Drake had ordered him to his knees as he pulled out a Smith & Wesson 9mm.

"I would never steal from Caine, Drake. You know that!"

"Your lies fall on deaf ears, L.J. We know you've stolen and you know the price."

As the word 'price' escaped Drake's lips, L.J. saw Caine, or more accurately, Caine's shadow enter the room. On his knees, in the middle of this room and with his head forced down by the barrel of the 9mm, he couldn't see anything that was higher than two feet off the floor. However, the width and height of the shadow - the sheer girth - combined with the situation that brought him here, told him all that he needed to know. It was Caine. That was when his bladder betrayed him and he peed himself.

He felt the barrel of the gun move away from his head, which was followed by an indecipherable, hushed conversation just a few feet away. It was the last thing L.J. ever heard. He never knew if it was Drake or Caine that stepped quietly to him, raised the gun to the back of his head and fired that fateful shot. The single shot barely registered with those that passed by at the time.

It would be nearly three weeks before the body was found.

[1] WINTER

MILWAUKEE - 17 MONTHS LATER

"Damn!" Marcus swore under his breath as he blew into his cupped hands, trying to warm them and fend off the cold October air. One day, not soon unfortunately, he would leave this city behind. As much as he loved catching the occasional Brewer's game in the spring, spending time at Lake Michigan in the summer and watching the Packers in the fall, he hated winters in Milwaukee, his hometown and the place he had called home all 20 years of his life. Absolutely hated it!

"What did you say?" asked Train.

"I hate the snow and it's too damn cold out here," Marcus told him, blowing more hot air into his cupped hands. "How much longer will we have to wait?" It was a rhetorical question of course. Like him, Train had no idea how much longer they would have to wait for Trevor, Marcus' supplier.

As he looked up and down the street, he thought about his most recent visit with his folks a few days ago. Of course, they had no knowledge of his side hustle. His brother did. His parents did not. They would be mortified if they knew. They only knew about the McDonald's thing. Though dinner that night was outstanding - as always - his father repeatedly pressed him on his plans now that he was out of high school. When was he going to get a better job? Was he saving money for college? Had he applied to any colleges yet? What majors was he considering?

He answered as he always did. "Right now I'm just getting my money together. I plan on going to college, but I don't want to be burdened with a ton of debt right out of the gate." Marcus loved his father; however, the cramped living space wasn't the only reason he moved out right after finishing high school.

The constant barrage from his father was too much. He was the type of person who just didn't know when enough was enough. As always, his mother gently rebuked her husband.

"Robert, you leave Marcus be. He's fine. He's a young man that has time to figure things out. He doesn't need to plot out the next 30 years in the next 30 days."

"That's true," his father replied. "However, he doesn't want to wake up

10 years from now wondering where the time went."

They followed dinner with a game of Dominoes, the Mexican Train version. Along with Scrabble, it was a family favorite. Although there was a lot of trash talking and the competitive juices were always flowing, there was more laughing and a sense of family cohesiveness during these times. *There really is something to the idea that a family that plays together, stays together,* Marcus mused.

Following the short game with his folks and younger brother, Marlon, he headed out, hoping he wouldn't miss the 7:25 p.m. bus. "How ya doin' tonight?" Marcus asked as he boarded the bus. The driver smiled and gave a slight nod. On the ride home through downtown, in between thoughts about what his future might hold, Marcus had glanced out windows with their frosted edges at some of the city's older buildings and their cream colored bricks.

Unlike a lot of people, even some of Milwaukee's longtime residents, Marcus knew the real story behind the city's nickname. While many mistakenly believed "Cream City" referred to the State's pre-eminence in the dairy industry, Marcus understood that the moniker was derived from the cream-colored bricks from which many of the city's buildings, particularly the older buildings, were constructed. One of the properties of the red clay that runs along the western shore of Lake Michigan is that it contains elevated amounts of sulfur and lime, and when formed into bricks, the rich clay turned a light golden yellow color after firing. Cream City indeed.

Cold and a little tired, Marcus' patience was wearing thin. "I might as well do something constructive with my time," Marcus called back as he started walking toward the corner. "Keep an eye out for Trevor, I'm gonna make a quick run over to the M&I Bank. I'll be back in 10 minutes."

"What do you need to do at the bank?" Train called out after a minute, but it was too late. Marcus was just out of earshot. Walking quickly, he was hoping Tracy was working this afternoon.

Walking into the bank and shaking off the cold, Marcus spotted her. Other than an older couple talking to one of the loan officers, not much was going on. The place was just about empty. Pausing before heading to the customer service counter, he grabbed his phone to check a new text message: *from Trevor – be there in 10.* Putting his phone away and stepping to the counter, he spoke first. "How are you Ms. Tracy on this cold, cold afternoon?" he asked as he approached her.

"Very well, Mr. Williams. How can I assist you today?" She was always so formal. Instead of being frustrated by her formality, Marcus found it endearing. A true professional.

"I just need to make a deposit, thank you." He tried to chat her up a little, but she was having none of it. As always, she offered him her very best customer service smile throughout the transaction and dutifully handed him his receipt for the deposit. However, he did see what he believed was the slightest sign of a real smile at the corner of her mouth when he assured her he would be back. She hadn't seen the last of him. Not by a long shot. "Take care, Ms. Tracy, and enjoy the rest of your day," he said as he turned and headed for the door.

Exactly 10 minutes after he had left, Marcus reappeared.

"What did you need to take care of?" Train inquired.

"I needed to make a deposit. The final deposit to get my emergency fund right."

"Your emergency what?" Train asked with a quizzical look on his face.

"My emergency fund. You know, we talked about the fund before," Marcus reminded him. "It's the money I keep in a savings account just for emergencies or to meet unexpected expenses. Should something out of the ordinary come up, I won't need to dip into the money I'm saving for college and retirement. My goal has always been to maintain $3,500, about three months of living expenses, in the account. I just hit the goal with the $150 I just deposited. I'm good now."

"How does ...?" Train started to say, just as they spotted Trevor.

As they made eye contact, Marcus drifted back into the alley where they should be able to get some privacy and a dilapidated awning would provide a little cover from the falling snow.

"How long ya'll been out here in the cold?" Trevor asked as he turned into the alley.

"Not long," Marcus lied as Train briefly glanced back and then resumed slowly scanning the street left to right. Perhaps not surprisingly, considering the nature of their work, Trevor was always a little paranoid. He claimed they had to meet out here because he was in the process of moving to a new apartment and he was late because he had to run down some former clients, looking for some money they owed. Who knew the real story?

As long as he had known him, Marcus only believed about half of what fell out of Trevor's mouth. That was okay though because he always came through with the goods and his prices were reasonable. His product, a nice strain of Afghan Kush, was reasonably priced, very potent and clients loved

4

it. Briefly they talked about their predictions for the Packers game that weekend, when the Bears would come calling.

"Packers in a blow-out, 31 - 10," Trevor proclaimed.

"I don't know," said Marcus. "The Bears defense is a little beat up and we have a superior offense, but I don't know if the Pack is 21 points better. My guess is it will be closer, maybe 24 - 17." As the temperature continued to drop and the snow started to let up, they concluded their transaction and prepared to part ways. "See you in a couple weeks," Marcus said as they turned to go in opposite directions.

"Yep, a couple weeks," Trevor replied.

Walking along North 21st Street with Train, in their Avenues West neighborhood, the two friends represented quite the contrast. Tall, with an athletic build, shallow dimples in both cheeks, a strong jaw line and clean shaven; it surprised many that Marcus had never considered modeling. Conversely, Train was considerably shorter, more pudgy than fat, and liked to maintain a tuft of hair - sort of like a black cotton ball - on his chin which he lovingly referred to as a 'chin-fro.' As they walked, Marcus' relaxed demeanor, warm smile and new Chuck Taylors wouldn't suggest he had $1,000 worth of weed and $500 cash stashed in his pockets and the lining of his coat.

With his supply replenished and Sal's Pizza coming into view, Marcus started thinking about when he first started this hustle. He was so damn naive. He didn't really know how or where to start. The only thing he knew for certain was that he was going to college and he couldn't make the money necessary working fast-food, part-time. An older friend, Redd, who had recently got out of the game, told him the most critical items were a scale and a phone. He had a phone, he needed a digital scale. Redd suggested either a Vitra or Ohaus. Both made quality scales at reasonable prices. Marcus decided to go with an Ohaus.

"The main thing," Redd said, "is make sure it can read down to tenths."

With a phone and scale in hand, he needed some startup capital. Although he had a little bit of money put away, he had to borrow the rest from his boy, Train. With the foundation in place, he was ready to find a supplier. Again, Redd came through. He was the conduit to Trevor. Within a week he was cultivating customers. His first group of clients were mainly fellow students at school. At that time it was a small customer base and he wasn't moving a lot of product. He was definitely small time.

However, once he moved to the Avenues West neighborhood, he picked up a lot of Marquette and Aurora Sinai Center clients and the business grew. Because of the neighborhood's diverse population, his customer base included people from all walks of life. In a typical day, it was not unusual for him to cater to blacks, whites, Hispanics, students, college professors and a host of young professionals.

As Train opened the door to Sal's, Marcus nonchalantly stole a peek behind him. It always paid to be mindful of your surroundings - the who and the what. Marcus understood all too well that the drug business favors extreme risk-takers, those who were willing to make gambles few other people, even the professionals on Wall Street, could handle. However, he knew it wasn't a career. You don't hear any stories about guys spending 20 years engaged in this lifestyle and then retiring to Miami Beach with their wife, 2.5 kids and dogs in tow. At least he hadn't.

Stay too long in the game and you likely ended up dead, in jail or maybe worse, like being paralyzed. That's what happened to Flex, a would be dealer on his way to being a bodybuilder. He caught a bullet in the back during a deal gone bad. "This isn't something I plan to do forever," Marcus told Train as they dipped into Sal's Pizza. The smell of fresh baked bread, the hint of garlic lingering in the air and the restaurant's warmth immediately enveloped Marcus. "People always get caught. Someone rats you out or you get stupid and sell something in the wrong place, at the wrong time."

"Or the wrong place at the right time," Train offered.

"Yep. No doubt."

Over a couple slices, the old friends reminisced about their days at South Division High School, home of the Cardinals.

"You were such a good student, always in them books. I always thought you'd find a way to go to college right after we graduated," said Train.

"Was never in the cards," Marcus responded. "My parents were never in a position to save money for college and there was no way I was going to take out a bunch of student loans. I should have looked into potential grants, but never took the time. I was considering joining the Army, even went to see that Army Recruiter over on North Oakland and took that ASVAB test. Did pretty well too. Also took the physical, but since I took Ritalin when I was younger, I couldn't join and get that college money through the G.I. Bill."

"What about takin' out some loans?" asked Train.

"No way, kid," Marcus responded as he lifted a slice of pepperoni pizza to his mouth, hoping its warmth would migrate through his body, knocking the chill off." I read something not too long ago that said the average cost of a college education had risen four times as fast as the rate of inflation.

"What!?" said Train. "That's crazy!"

"That it is, my friend" said Marcus as he shook his head. "I will definitely get my college degree, but I won't become a slave to debt to do it. Too many people out there graduating with degrees that won't get 'em a job making enough money to pay back the loans they took out for the degree. Ain't gonna be me. My plan is to get some type of engineering degree, which should make me employable, and leave college with just the degree and not all that debt hanging over my head." Finishing up their pizza and the last of their drinks, they paid, slipped into their coats and prepared to face the cold.

"Peace," Marcus offered as they left Sal's. It had started to snow again as Train headed west to meet his girl, Renee, while Marcus headed north toward North 14th Street to make a delivery to Eric, a longtime customer. If the opportunity to sell a portion of his two week supply to other dealers presented itself, he often took it. He would rather go for a quick turnaround and a small profit if possible. However, he didn't mind if the opportunity wasn't there. Ultimately his success was tied to maintaining his client base, currently around 65 people, and keeping them happy.

While most of the dealers in his neighborhood dealt only on the street, Marcus was unusual in that he dealt on the street as well as delivering to the homes of some of his more well-heeled clients, a practice he started a little over a year ago, after graduating. He figured it made sense to move into other forms of distribution, to expand his client base. It always struck Marcus as somewhat amusing that these clients would place an order for drugs to be delivered to their apartments as casually as if they would order Thai food.

Approaching the open apartment door, Marcus caught Eric's eye. Dressed in a dark suit and a bold tie, as if he had just left a high-powered meeting, Eric motioned for Marcus to come in as he remained engaged in his phone conversation. Speaking softly, Marcus asked, "Why is your door open? It's cold out there," as he stepped in and closed the door behind him. Cupping his hand over the phone and speaking in a low whisper, "I figured you'd be here any minute," Eric replied. Marcus already knew what the man wanted. As a regular, he had texted his order ahead of time using a pre-determined pattern of messages. Unlike his street deals, which were often consummated on the spot, Marcus communicated and verified most of his business with his more well-heeled customers via text messages.

If an established customer, like Eric, had friends who wanted to make use of Marcus' services, those new clients were introduced via a text message. The practice ensured new referrals came strictly from within trusted social circles, by way of friends who would vouch for the weed's quality. That way, his customers ended up acting not only as a sort of advertising service, but it also provided a measure of security to everybody involved.

It was quite the contrast from dealing on the street where most of his deals were handled on the spot with no prior arrangement and security was essentially non-existent. Hell, Train wasn't always around. Though he dealt on the street, he wasn't a fool. He rotated between different spots and under no circumstances did he deal in parking lots. While it might be easier to agree to meet someone in the parking lot of a retail store, it was a bad idea in the age of video surveillance. Anybody that dealt in lots was just waiting to get caught.

He also did his best to stay clear of Neighborhood Watch groups. The most active one in this neighborhood was in the 18th Street to 20th Street three block area. The Watch Leader, Mr. Pemberton, didn't play. He took the renovation and revitalization effort of Avenues West very seriously. The Neighborhood Watch was his contribution to the effort. That area was best avoided. At the end of the day, by working two distinctive niches, he increased his customer base, which meant more money, which meant the sooner he could get out of the game and on to his life.

Marcus reached into the inside pocket of his coat and pulled out three baggies, Eric's regular order. Eric wrapped up his conversation and greeted Marcus with an awkward fist bump and "What's up, bro?"

Why did it always have to be, 'bro?' Marcus was pretty sure he didn't greet all males that way. They spoke briefly, Eric bemoaning the recent downturn in the stock market, 3% over the last week, and Marcus bemoaning the cold weather.

"The damn Fed is making a mess of the economy and fucking up the stock market! It's hard enough trying to figure out what and when to trade and nearly impossible when you throw in that damn quantitative easing. They're killing me!"

Finished with the requisite chit chat, Eric handed over his money and Marcus headed for the door. It probably would have come as a surprise to Eric, but Marcus was quite aware that the market had been down lately. Unlike the vast majority of dealers, in this town or others, he was quite familiar with the stock market. In fact, he was thinking this might be a good time to pick up more shares of the one stock he owned, Netflix, and maybe make an extra contribution to his IRA account.

Moving onto his next appointment, two bags for a chiropractor three blocks to the east, Marcus started thinking more about the proposal he had heard earlier on MSNBC. In a strange pairing, Rand Paul, the libertarian leaning Republican from Kentucky and Cory Booker, the moderate Democrat from New Jersey, freshmen senators both, were teaming up to introduce a comprehensive overhaul of the nation's criminal justice system. Elements of their REDEEM Act recognized that the War on Drugs had largely been a failure and a new approach was needed.

Combining that development with public statements by Attorney General Eric Holder advocating for commuting drug sentences and the fact that there were now two states (Colorado and Washington) where weed was legal, and 18 more where it was decriminalized, or approved for medical use, it seemed pretty clear to Marcus that there was a seismic shift underway.

Savvy dealers understood that a new environment - one in which knowledge of specific strains of the plant and medicinal applications would replace the need for sheer chutzpah - and a new type of entrepreneur may soon cut them out of the picture. For dealers like Marcus, this was quickly becoming a muddled time to be in this line of work. No doubt the sooner he got out, the better. "Yep, the sooner I get out of this town, and this cold-ass weather, the better," he mumbled to himself as he pulled his Packers knit cap out of his pocket and hunkered down into his coat. *Damn, it was cold!*

[2] THE GRIND

Although you will find some working-class families and elderly residents in the Johnson Square Apartments, the majority of the residents are unemployed - or underemployed - single mothers. When he moved in a little over a year ago Marcus wasn't the only weed dealer in Johnson Square, just the latest. Multiple dealers worked the Square. However, once he moved in, things began to change. Marcus knew early on he would have to get creative and out-hustle them. In this game, the early and late bird got the worm.

The first few months he worked the hours nobody else would. Anybody could work 8:00 a.m. to 10:00 p.m. Not many were willing to burn the midnight oil and be hustling, especially when it's cold, at 2:00, 3:00, and 4:00 in the morning. Initially, to draw in new customers and peel away some from the competition, he offered discounted samples. Not free, but discounted.

His strategy worked. Within a few months, he had built up a sizable client base, driven out some of the low performing competition and clearly established himself as the top weed dealer in the area. He didn't believe that was necessarily anything to be proud of. After all, his ambition was not to be the best drug dealer he could be. However, the end - if not justified - was served by the means.

Startled awake by the blare of his alarm clock, Marcus rolled over and smacked the snooze button. Seven minutes later, although he wanted to hit snooze again, he hit the off button instead. Wiping the sleep from his eyes, he sat up and let his feet fall to the floor. He knew it was going to be a long one, but he was ready to face the day. He was scheduled for the mid-morning shift and only had about two hours before he had to be at work. Walking, stretching and yawning, he headed to the kitchen to get a glass of water.

If he hustled he would have just enough time for a quick three-mile run and a fruit and vegetable smoothie for breakfast. He didn't want to press his luck with Vanessa, the store manager, this morning. He could hear her now, "Late again, Marcus, you're going on probation!" Though the pay sucked, he needed the money and there weren't a lot of options out there for a brotha with just a high school diploma. You didn't need a degree in economics to know that the economy wasn't producing good, full-time jobs and if you were smart, you held onto the one you had. *Yep*, he thought to himself, *be there on time, be productive and keep your head low. Just like the weed hustle, working McDonald's was a means to an end.*

Although he was not satisfied with his $7.55 an hour job at McDonalds, $0.30 above the state's minimum wage, the job was another activity that served the greater purpose. While he was sympathetic to the cause, he wasn't about to join any of the protests. Two of his co-workers participated in the rally last December over at the store on West North Avenue. Stood out in the cold and held up their homemade signs, 'Living Wage = $15/Hour.'

No doubt that you couldn't make ends meet on minimum wage. However, he didn't see any way these fast-food corporations, or their franchisees, were going to pay anywhere near the $15 an hour that was being demanded. And accepting unions? Wasn't gonna happen. Anyway, between working 25 -30 hours a week at Mickey D's and putting in time on his side hustle, he didn't have the time to spare at a protest. Hell, he certainly wasn't going to make fast-food a career. Not only would it not be a career, he was planning to be done with McDonald's and Milwaukee within the next year.

Stepping out his front door, the cool air engulfed his head causing his eyes to reflexively squint. He had half a mind to turn around and grab another 30 minutes of sleep. He knew better though. He knew he had to stay physically fit, just as he was making moves to get financially fit. After pulling down his knit cap a little and slipping on his lightweight running gloves, he stretched briefly. Nothing too intense. He had heard that more people injured themselves before a physical activity by trying to stretch too hard before the muscles warmed up; particularly in cold weather. And this was definitely cold weather.

Taking off at a leisurely pace, he settled into a nice rhythm after a few minutes and started to warm up a little. At this time of day there weren't a lot of people out in the hood, just a few folks headed to work, either making their way to the bus stop or making the short walk if they worked close enough. Though cold, it was a nice crisp morning and it felt good to be up and active.

Turning for home he ran past Carl, one of his first steady customers.
"Can you square me away today?" Carl called out. Running short on breath, "Gotta do that 9:00 to 5:00," (which was really 7:00 to 12:00 in his case), Marcus shot back. "I'll be around about 1:00."

Picking up the pace for the last ¼ mile, Marcus felt his heart rate rise and the first trickle of sweat fell into his eye as he approached the Square. Slowing to a walk, he took some deep breaths as he made his way to his apartment door. Though he was a little tired, he felt good. *I have never regretted a workout when I was finished. Although some go better than others, it always felt good to get a workout in,* he thought to himself. After a quick shower, a smoothie and watering his plants, he grabbed his backpack and was out the door.

Nine minutes later he was on the bus headed to work. Rolling through the front door with three minutes to spare, he gave Vanessa his best fake smile, kind of like Tracy at the bank, with her customer service smile.

"You're on drive-thru, Marcus," Vanessa informed him as he walked by. That was fine with him. Although it was a little more intense than working the grill or front counter, Marcus liked the pressure of ensuring the orders were accurate and each customer was taken care of within 90 seconds from the time they placed their order. At least that was the goal.

Working under the gun helped the day go by faster. It was also good that he was working with Antoine, probably the person he got along with best here at work. Antoine had graduated a couple years before Marcus, worked at the store for three years and had recently been promoted to shift manager.

"How's that promotion working out, man? You like working with Vanessa?" Marcus asked when there was a lull in the action.

"She's alright," Antoine responded. "As long as people get to work on time and don't abuse their breaks, she stays pretty cool. She definitely knows what it takes to run the place. I didn't realize there were so many little things to pay attention to; so many things to consider when running a store." Taking advantage of the lull, Marcus let Antoine know he was going to take his 10-minute break. Unlike a lot of his co-workers, he wasn't interested in grabbing a smoke. He used his breaks to stay on top of the side hustle.

Two of his co-workers were regular customers and Marcus noticed that one of them, Maria, had just headed out for a break. More importantly, the six or seven vibrations from his phone throughout the morning told him there were some clients reaching out. Two were from Train - he had to catch up with him later - one was from his moms and three were from clients. After checking the messages, he caught up with Maria around back. They made a quick exchange on a single bag, making sure not to draw any unnecessary attention and before anyone else came around back.

Lighting up a menthol, she asked, "When we gon' hook up?" The question caught him a little off-guard, but he'd known for awhile that Maria had a thing for him. However, he was too busy with work. All his work. She was attractive - with a nice round backside - and had a good sense of humor, but she was kind of a drama queen and he didn't have the patience for it. Plus, he didn't really care for the smoking thing and of course, there was Tracy.

"You know me, girl. I'm too busy right now. Trying to work, hustle and figure out the college thing."

"Maybe I can squeeze you into my schedule in a couple weeks," he joked.

"Alright, Mr. Man, you let me know when you can find some time," she said between long, deep drags. "When you're able, block off a date and time in your little day planner for me."

As Maria stepped off to make a call, Marcus chuckled, "Will do Ms. Ramirez. Will do." The next order of business was to respond to his text messages, setting up drop-off times. With that done, he took in a few deep breaths of the cool air and headed back inside. Walking back inside, *Happy* by Pharrell Williams popped into his head and he started humming the tune. That song was like Ebola or something. Once it got into you, it was hard to shake loose.

The rest of his shift went pretty smoothly, even the normally hectic transition from the breakfast menu to the lunch menu at 10:30 a.m. He managed to stay out of Vanessa's crosshairs and a half hour before his shift ended, the second co-worker, Pete, who was a regular customer, showed up for his. Crossing paths going in and out of the men's room, they managed a seamless transaction of two bags.

Walking out the door after changing and clocking out, Marcus threw on his headphones, checked his phone - four more messages - and picked up a slow jog to make sure he didn't miss the next bus. He had to put in some time back on the block and he had multiple house calls to make later that afternoon. He didn't have time to be sittin' around at a bus stop, just waiting. Time was money. At least that was what Benjamin Franklin said. He was pretty sure it was Benjamin Franklin. Or was it Thomas Jefferson? It was one of them dudes.

Stepping off the bus, Marcus ran into Carl as he was approaching his apartment complex. Tall, every bit of 6'8" and lanky, he was hard to miss. Marcus had heard Carl used to be quite the ball player at Marquette back in the day. Had to be way back in the day! His guess was that Carl hadn't even touched a basketball in 20 years.

"What up, young man?" the old-timer wanted to know. "Need to head upstairs first?" Carl asked. Reaching into his pocket, "Nope," Marcus replied as they quickly conducted business. And just like that, Carl was on his way. Lurching down the street to who knew where. Before he had a chance to get upstairs and change clothes, two more regulars approached him. Busy, busy, busy.

Glancing around as he quickly conducted his transactions, he noticed a new face. Giving him a long, hard stare, the stranger made it clear he was not interested in minding his own business, or conducting any with Marcus. Holding his gaze, Marcus followed his movement up the street until he rounded the corner. Marcus had been in the game, and this neighborhood, long enough to know when it was 5-0 and when it was some other form of danger. The new face definitely wasn't 5-0, which meant there was a good chance he was some other kind of danger. What kind, he didn't know. Marcus had taken a mental snapshot of the new face and he made a mental note to speak to Train, see if he could run down any information.

Before he got tied up any longer, he rushed upstairs, taking two steps at a time to the second floor, changed and sent a text message: *to Train – hit me back when you have a min we need to talk.* Walking over to the printer in the corner of the living room, he released the obscure latch on the back. Hollowed out, it served as a pretty good hiding place for his weed. He wasn't crazy about the idea of keeping the weed in his apartment; however, he felt more comfortable with it here instead of someplace else. Double-bagged and vacuum sealed, he figured it was as good a spot as any.

Grabbing 20 baggies, he transferred them into his backpack and headed out the door to make his deliveries. All dealers knew you tried to avoid carrying around small baggies, with or without weed in them. If ever stopped, multiple baggies indicated intent to sell. Like a lot of states, good old Wisconsin didn't play when it came to intent to sale. If he was not mistaken, the cultivation or intent to distribute 200 grams or less included a fine of up to $10,000 and up to three and half years in prison. "Yep, serious business," he whispered under his breath.

When multiple deliveries needed to be made, a trip home between each sale was worth it when it could mean the difference between a misdemeanor or a felony. Even though he understood the potential ramifications, he had too many deliveries to make, over too large an area, so he was going to have to take his chances. He didn't have time to run back to his place between every sale, or even every two sales.

No sooner had he walked out his front door, turned the corner, headed toward North 18th to meet Train, when he spotted Gwen, a former client, across the street. Bowing his head and picking up the pace, he hoped she wouldn't see him. She had been blowing up his phone lately trying to get back onto his good side. He had four cardinal rules that he absolutely enforced, no exceptions. Break one of the rules - get busted, ask for other drugs, constantly pester or show up unannounced - and you had to find a new dealer.

If a client got busted, even if it wasn't their fault, they were toxic. Kind of like that black mold. Who knew what deals may have been made with 5-0 or if they were still being watched. Once busted, Marcus didn't want to be seen with them under any circumstances. Marcus prided himself on being strictly a marijuana dealer. None of that other shit. No rock, no meth, no pills, no smack. Once a client started soliciting him for heavier drugs, it was time to cut them off.

Text him more than a couple of times a day, soon he would cut you off. He didn't appreciate being pestered. Once he indicated he would get to you, he would. A barrage of text messages and constant pestering wasn't gonna make it happen any sooner. He didn't have time for people who couldn't practice patience.

The most sacred of his rules was showing up unannounced. Marcus learned early on that limiting foot traffic was one of the keys to not getting busted. Moreover, he simply didn't like people showing up at this doorstep, at the place he used to escape the things out on the street. The place he laid his head at night. He only gave permission to a few trusted clients, who had unique situations, to visit him at his apartment. Everyone else knew it was strictly prohibited. No exceptions. None! Over the years, Marcus had experienced each of his rules being broken by a client. Gwen's mistake was getting busted.

No luck, she spotted him quickly.

"Yo, Marcus, let me holler at you for a minute," she called out as she crossed the street, breaking into a slow trot. And Gwen, at a slow trot with those massive titties, was not a sight soon forgotten.

"What up, Gwen? How you been?"

"You know, just trying to stay employed, make rent and live life. I sure the hell ain't livin' the American dream. Why haven't you been returning my calls or responding to my text messages? I've been a loyal customer, never caused you no headaches."

"True," Marcus agreed. "However, like I said before, once someone gets busted, I can't work with them anymore. It's too dangerous. You know how this works."

"Man, I hate trying to score from Freddy. His prices are too damn high, the quality is shit and he's always hard to get a hold of."

He really didn't have a good response for her. "Look, Gwen, I really gotta go. I'm running late and Train is waiting on me. Let me give it some thought and I'll let you know. Quit blowing up my phone though. Please. I'll reach out to you. Cool?" With that, she headed back across the street and Marcus picked up his pace. "Damn, I hate running late," he cursed under his breath. While he hated to mislead people, he had no intention of taking Gwen back on as a client. With any luck she would lose his number and find another source. Or both if he was lucky.

If nothing else, eventually she would get the message and stop contacting him. You had to be careful. Scorned customers could be your worst enemy. They know where you deal, who you run with, everything. It wouldn't take much for one to get mad and rat you out to 5-0. On second thought, maybe he would let her back in the fold. Who knew? He couldn't worry about it right now. Just then he got a message: *from Train - can't make it 2night renee's fussin' about spending some time.*

Damn, he thought to himself. *I really wanted to run my encounter past Train. See what he thought.* Oh well, they'd have to hook up later. It looked like he was on his own.

Eight deliveries that afternoon. Based on the various locations, he figured the most efficient way to hit all eight in the shortest period of time would be to start with Robert and finish with Estelle. That worked out nice since he liked spending a little time with Estelle. They always had good conversations and she always gave him something new to think about. A white, sixty-something grandmother, she certainly wasn't the stereotypical weed user. You certainly wouldn't see her face on the evening news when they were presenting a profile of a typical user. More likely, it would be a face like his. Black and young. However, she suffered from a lot of lower back pain and like a lot of people who appreciated the medicinal qualities, she swore by the drug.

Getting through the first seven deliveries without any drama and making good time, Marcus headed to Estelle's, over on North 26th Street. Turning the corner, he thought he caught a glimpse of the stranger from earlier that day reflected off the plate glass window of the Dollar Store. Glancing back quickly, he didn't see anything. Maybe, like Trevor, he was getting a little paranoid. Stay in this game long enough and that would certainly be the case. A few steps later, he shot a quick glance over his left shoulder. Nothing. His paranoia satisfied, he rubbed his hands together for some quick warmth and continued on to Estelle's.

As was customary, she offered him a cup of coffee soon after he had taken his coat off, placed her two baggies on the kitchen counter and settled on the couch. He normally only had one cup of coffee a day in the morning, maybe two. He could never refuse her offer though.

"How are things going?" she asked. "Anything new happening at McDonald's?"

"Not really," he replied. "Just trying to keep my head low and stay out of Vanessa's crosshairs." She knew as well as he did that keeping the Mickey D's job was paramount. Not only was it a source of income for funding his savings and investment accounts, all kind of suspicions would be raised if he was steadily contributing to the accounts with no legally recognized employment.

"If all goes as planned, I will be ready to quit that job and make my move within a year." She was aware of his emergency fund, so he shared that he had recently made the final deposit to reach his savings account goal.

"Congratulations!" she said. "Too many people underestimate the importance of a solid emergency fund and end up using credit cards when the unexpected, or unplanned, happens. I know it happened to me on more than one occasion when I was younger. Seems like 100 years ago." Marcus laughed, almost spitting out a mouthful of coffee.

"Combine that with buying too much shit they don't need on credit and debt becomes a serious issue. You'll never reach your goals if you're constantly struggling to pay for products or services you bought years ago." Marcus chuckled a little as it was rare to hear Estelle curse, even a pretty tame curse word such as 'shit.' He couldn't even imagine the 'F' Bomb falling out of her mouth. That would be too much. Way too much.

The conversation about debt made him think of the Will Rogers quote, "Too many people spend money they haven't earned, to buy things they don't want, to impress people that they don't like." Too true! They chatted for another 15 minutes or so, about the weather, and the Packers of course, as Marcus prepared to make his exit. Train had texted while they were talking and he really needed to talk to his friend about his encounter earlier with the stranger.

As he began to excuse himself Estelle said, "Just a minute. I will be right back." A few minutes later she returned with a small medallion on a silver chain.

"What is that?" he asked.

"This is a Saint Joseph medallion. Not only was he the husband of Mary and the stepfather of Jesus, he is the Patron Saint of work and workers. As you go about your work, in an effort to pay for college and secure your financial future, may he watch over you."

"It belonged to my son. You have been very kind to me. The marijuana provides me great relief, and more importantly, I have come to very much appreciate your friendship and our conversations. As you put forth the effort to reach a better place, you may need a little luck here and there. I hope this provides it," she said as she handed it to him.

"Thank you," Marcus said. "I don't know what to say. I know this means a great deal to you. I'm touched. It has been a long time since someone gave me anything."

After they exchanged a long hug, he excused himself and thanked Estelle for the coffee and the Saint Joseph medallion. She had told him previously about her son, who died in a car accident at the age of 23. It meant a great deal to him that she thought enough of him to entrust him with it. She thanked him for the weed and the company.

"Take care, Sweetie," she said as he walked out the door, heading over to Qdoba Mexican Grill to meet Train.

[3] CAINE

Grabbing a corner table, Marcus and Train sat down with their large burritos and sides of pico de gallo and guacamole. Marcus began by describing the situation. "I was conducting business down the street from the apartment when I glanced up and noticed a new face. It wasn't so much the fact that it wasn't someone who was familiar to me, it was the fact he gave me a real hard, long stare. It was clear that he wasn't interested in conducting business. It was more like he was sizing me up, for what I don't know."

Before Marcus could start describing him, Train jumped in. "What did he look like?"

"A dark-skinned brotha, a little shorter than me, kinda stocky and bald with a goatee with clean lines. Seen him around?"

"Doesn't sound familiar. What was he wearing?"

"Some dark boots, maybe Doc Martens, baggy jeans and an old, faded Army coat. I think they call them field jackets," Marcus responded without a moment's hesitation.

"Hmm, nothing," Train said. "The description doesn't sound familiar, but I'll keep my ear to the ground and talk to some people, see what they know."

"Switching gears for a minute, man, let's go back to that whole emergency thing."

"You mean the emergency fund?" Marcus interrupted him.

"Yeah, man. It seems like every time we talk, you get me to thinkin' about my money or thinkin' about it in a new way. I know you had mentioned something before when we were talking about building a financial foundation, but I don't remember that piece."

"Like I said before, it's the money kept in a savings account just for emergencies or to meet unexpected expenses. Should something out of the ordinary come up, you don't need to dip into the money earmarked for savings and investing. As an example, remember last year when I had to replace the brakes on my car?"

"Yeah, I remember."

"Well of course I ended up getting rid of it, but at the time I thought I was going to keep it for a long while. Too many issues though. Better to cut my losses and sell it. Instead of using money intended for my savings and investments, I just pulled the money out of the savings account where I maintain my emergency fund."

"One of the first rules of personal finance that I came across is that you should pay yourself first, meaning, do things like build an emergency fund and contribute to your savings and investment accounts before anything else: paying bills, going out to dinner, going to the movies, buying new clothes, buying a new cell phone, everything else. You'll never get around to meeting your financial goals if your income is constantly diverted to other obligations. The worst is credit card debt. Too many people turn to using credit cards to not only buy stuff they don't need, but to cover emergencies also. They end up spending money that could have gone to meeting a financial goal to make payments on credit cards with those high-ass interest rates."

"I've seen plenty of that," Train agreed.

"My immediate goal is to save enough money to start college and my secondary goal is to build the foundation for my retirement nest-egg. According to the Department of Education, two years at a community college - where I plan to start, keeping the cost lower - is about $18,000 on average. The last two years at a university will run about double that. Therefore, I'm probably looking at somewhere around $54,000."

"Damn, that's a lot of money!" Train proclaimed.

"No doubt, man." I'm not trying to get it all at once though. I figure if I can have two-thirds of it, $36,000, saved before starting at a community college, I can work part-time while I'm going to school. That should put me in a nice position to finish without any student loans, without the heavy burden of debt."

"How close are you to the $36,000?"

"I'm at $21,489.85. Just over $14,000 to go."

"What about that retirement money? How is that going?" Train inquired.

"Not too bad. I opened an IRA account last year and I've been steadily making monthly contributions of $100. So I'm at about $1,000. Once my education is paid for, I will be in a position to contribute a little bit more until I get to the point where I can contribute the maximum."

Was it difficult opening an account, hiring one of them financial advisors and everything?"

"Nope. A lot of people don't realize you can go through good companies like Fidelity or Vanguard and open the account yourself in a matter of minutes. No need to pay somebody to do something you can do yourself." Basically, the accounts that are forming my financial foundation are in place. My savings accounts for the emergency fund and college; and my investment account for my IRA are all set. Now, it's all about funding them."

"As long as I can get through the next year or so without any drama associated with dealing weed, like that shit over on West Capitol Drive the other night, I don't see a problem hittin' my goals and then making my move.

"What drama?" asked Train.

"You didn't read about that shit in the paper or hear about it on the news?"

"Nope," said Train as he shook his head from side to side.

"You need to read a paper or check the news once in awhile, my brotha. Find out what's going on in the space around you."

Apparently, a couple of days ago, in the middle of the afternoon, like 2:00, some fool named Q-Ball, now there's a name for ya, and several of his partners went looking for this dude named Redbone and ran across him on Capitol Drive. They exchanged some words and then just like that, Q-Ball broke out his piece and shot Redbone twice. Once in the shoulder and once in the thigh. They say all hell really broke loose after that. Witnesses said gunfire exploded from damn near every direction. Hard as it is to believe, they say nobody died, although that Redbone was shot up pretty good. A bunch of kids was in the area, but thankfully, none of 'em got hit. It can be crazy out here, man."

"Let me know what you can find out on the dude I described. Something wasn't right with him."

"Like I said, the description doesn't sound familiar, but I'll keep my ear to the ground and talk to some people, see what they know," Train assured him.

"Appreciate it, man."

Getting back to the house Drake hustled past the new guard, Ricky, stopping at the kitchen - transformed into a packaging area - and spoke briefly with Tanisha, head of packaging. "Got everything you need?" he asked. "How ya looking on supplies?"

"We got everything we need for now. Probably gonna need more baggies in a few days and it probably wouldn't hurt if we had another scale. Maybe pick up an Ohaus. They're good scales." He added the items to his mental shopping list.

"Gotcha," he assured her. Lowering his voice, he asked, "How the new people working out? You see any potential issues?"

"Nope. Everything and everybody looks real cool so far."

"Good. We don't have time for personality conflicts or some other Mickey Mouse bullshit."

This shit is crazy, just like something out of New Jack City or a number of other gangster movies, Drake thought to himself as he made his way to the back room where Michael spent most of his time. An enterprise looking at potentially $3M annually and naked bitches preparing drugs for distribution in a converted kitchen. Crazy. This life was damn crazy. He had to give it to his cousin, he had a way with numbers and he knew what he was doing. He was just along for the ride.

Cousins that grew up together, Drake and Michael were as close as brothers. That's why he was the only one that called him by his given name, or Mike, when they were alone. He typically resorted to using his street name, Caine, when around the staff. Those occasions were rare, however, as Drake was typically the one they dealt with and he was definitely the face of the enterprise to their suppliers and the dealer base they were putting into place. Earned in Chicago - where he cut his teeth in the drug game - Caine was proud of the name bestowed upon him, and the fact that in a mere four years, he had become the largest dealer of Cocaine in the city.

His interest in expanding beyond the drug from which his name was derived is what had brought him to Milwaukee. That would have been hard to do in the City of Bullets. On the other hand, Milwaukee, the so called Cream City, would be a much easier mountain to climb. He had thoroughly researched the Cream City prior to making his move. The city was dominated by three groups of distributors and two primary drugs, crack and marijuana.

African American gangs on the north side converted powder cocaine to crack in selected cook houses. When the cocaine supply ran low, they often bought from the Hispanic gangs who controlled the south side of the city. In various pockets throughout the city, Caucasian males were the typical distributors of weed, which they often grew in grow closets, which resembled stand-alone refrigerators but were actually self-contained cannabis grow sites. For Caine, the answer was to go west. West of the city. Bordered by I-43 on the east, 27th Street on the west, I-94 on the south, and by Highland Avenue to the north, Avenues West was his new home. His new playground. This is where he would make his money.

After decades of low income levels, stagnation and neglect, compounded by the housing crisis and economic downturn in 2008, Avenues West was one of Milwaukee's down-and-out neighborhoods that was on the rise. Slowly. Like many of the other residential districts ringing downtown, it was home to Milwaukee's predominantly working class, poor and minorities. These neighborhoods were home to thousands of blighted structures and abandoned lots; and where the oppressive weight of violent crime and poverty held its citizens down.

While income levels were still relatively low, they had risen a little and the area had seen some signs of redevelopment recently. Avenues West was fighting back. The old Ambassador Hotel over on West Wisconsin Avenue was a good example of that. It wasn't that long ago that prostitution and drug dealing were rampant in the run down place. Pimps and hoes everywhere. The restoration had started to change all that. Caine didn't have a problem with it being more of an upscale place after the renovation, he just wanted to do his part to bring some drugs to the people. After all, grown people should be able to do what grown people wanted to do.

Using Coke as his foundation, the plan was simple. Add meth, crack, weed, ecstasy and heroin to his portfolio and overtake one neighborhood at a time. His research indicated Avenues West was a good place to start and weed was the market he would corner first. They had bought this nondescript house on a nondescript, relatively quiet, block a few months ago. After getting the packaging area prepared and an adequate staff in place they were just about ready to put their plan into action.

As he stepped into the room, his cousin cut right to the chase. He was never much for small talk.

"What up, Cuz?" What can you tell me about the tall brotha that appears to be dealing most of the weed in Avenues West? You been watchin' him a little while now."

"His name is Marcus. Marcus Williams. He lives in that apartment complex over on West Wells and deals from three or four spots in the neighborhood. He plays it smart. Doesn't hang out at any one location for long, rotates his movements between the different spots and he doesn't deal out of his apartment."

"Anything else?" Caine asked.

"Yep. It also appears as if the street customers are just one part of his client base. He has in hands in multiple pots so to speak. He also makes home deliveries over in the Marquette and Medical Center area."

"Oh, really?" said Caine, more to himself and not really as a question for his cousin. "That's interesting."

"One more thing," Drake offered. His runnin' partner is a dude named Train. Apparently they go way back."

"Bring Mr. Williams to me. I want to talk to him, get a feel for him and see where his head's at."

Finishing up their burritos, Marcus and Train made a beeline for the exit. Although it was snowing lightly, it didn't feel too cold outside. It wasn't that bone chilling kind of cold, the kind you felt every time you took a step. The two friends headed towards Marcus' apartment. Marcus had to pick up some more product and he wanted to take care of a few local clients before they went to a movie. He had told them he would be around later that night. They weren't sure what they were gonna see yet, but it didn't really matter. It was just a good reason to grab some overpriced popcorn and chocolate covered raisins, kick their feet back and relax.

"What was Renee fussin' about earlier?"

"Not a lot, man. She was just a little upset that we haven't seen a lot of each other lately. As I tried to explain to her, sometimes it's hard when we're both working. The schedules don't always line up. So I just had to put in a little time."

Getting back to the Square, Marcus grabbed 10 baggies from his apartment and headed out to one of his spots. Within 45 minutes he had taken care of those he needed to and they were ready to go. "Anything?" he asked.

"Nope," replied Train who had been standing back at a distance, keeping an eye out for danger in general and the stranger Marcus described, specifically. All his baggies gone and with the movie starting in 30 minutes, they headed out. "You treatin' tonight?" Train asked. "I'm a little light on this fine evening."

"Hell boy, you're always light," Marcus chided him.

[4] THE STRANGER

Startled awake by the blare of his alarm clock, Marcus rolled over and smacked the snooze button. Seven minutes later, although he wanted to hit snooze again, he hit the off button instead. Wiping the sleep from his eyes, he sat up and let out a soft chuckle. If he didn't know any better, he'd swear he just had a *Groundhog Day* moment. The last few minutes seemed eerily familiar to yesterday morning. It was déjà vu all over again. Throwing his feet to the floor, he headed to the kitchen, stretching and yawning all the way. Yep, just like yesterday.

Today however, he was taking a day off from running. Instead, he turned on the television, flipping the channels until he got to Bloomberg TV. The financial news channel would serve as adequate background noise while he made his smoothie and got ready for work. First however, some push-ups and sit-ups. One hundred and fifty each, six sets of twenty-five, should do it.

Finishing up with the chest, triceps and ab work, Marcus sprang to his feet and washed his hands. As he threw some frozen blueberries into the blender, followed by a banana, a little Greek yogurt and a couple of apples, he listened in as one of the regular talking heads prognosticated about the market:

> "If you look at history, the bull markets do not end when the Fed starts raising interest rates. Bull markets could go on for another nine months to two years. Maybe it will be March or April instead of June or July. That should not matter at all, in terms of the big picture. The bull market is definitely not over. I still think the bull is taking control of this market. I don't think he's going to give up."

"What?" he asked incredulously to the empty room. Just a couple of days ago, another well respected, presumably knowledgeable investor, had literally guaranteed that the Bull Run was over and we were at the beginning of an extended Bear market. Well, one of them was going to be wrong. But of course, these would be Nostradamuses always offered a caveat, just enough room to wiggle out of any predictions. Ha, who could believe any of them?

With more time today, Marcus adopted a leisurely pace as he got ready.

After enjoying his smoothie he set about preparing his coffee. The first order of business was to fill the maker with four cups of cold, charcoal-filtered water. Next, two heaping scoops of Yuban Organic Medium Roast, his current favorite. Turning the coffee pot on, he grabbed his mug adding one teaspoon of sugar and one tablespoon of heavy whipping cream. It was the routine he performed every morning when he had time. Soon the intense aroma of plum blossom and black currant began to waft throughout the apartment.

Once the coffee was finished brewing he poured the black liquid into his favorite mug and watched as it morphed into a caramel colored nectar. Reaching for the remote, he changed the channel to CNBC to see what was going on over there. Apparently a panel was in the middle of a conversation with the President of Investment Strategies for a financial services company about geopolitical risks and the impacts to stock markets:

> Host: "Describe the relationship between geopolitical risks and the stock market."

> Guest: "The stock market often trades very well during crises. While crises such as Iraq, Russia and Syria do inject some anxiety, the market seems able to absorb the often bad news. Right now the NASDAQ is trading at a historically modest valuation and at the same time, the economy in the United States appears to be picking up a little steam. Perhaps more importantly, the auto manufacturers are rising. The improvements in the overall fundamentals seem to offset these short-term geopolitical stressors."

On and on the TV droned. Finishing up his coffee, he turned off the TV and laced up his shoes. Ten minutes before the bus was scheduled to arrive, he grabbed his backpack, wallet and keys and slipped out the door. The start to his workday got off to a promising start as the bus was right on time and he made it to work with 12 minutes to spare.

Looking around as he stepped through the door, he didn't see Vanessa. That was odd as it seemed like she was always here and always out on the floor or in the kitchen. In fact, now that he thought about it, he couldn't remember the last time he didn't see her at work. She was always here and he had never seen her take a break. Ever.

Taking off his coat, out of the corner of his eye he saw Antoine approaching him.

"I'm gonna need you to help me today," Antoine said, almost pleadingly. "Vanessa called in sick about 40 minutes ago and we've got two trainees in house today."

"Not a problem, we should be alright," Marcus assured him as he headed back toward the kitchen. He had no idea how wrong he would be.

Pretty much everything that could have gone wrong, did. Neither of the crew members on the front counter could not get it together, the trainees were getting in the way more than anything else - in fact, one ended up quitting later that day - one of the grills was not heating properly and to make matters worse, the breakfast crowd was larger than normal. You would have thought somebody told all these people free hash browns were being given away. And whereas the transition from the breakfast menu to the lunch menu went smoothly yesterday, that definitely was not the case today.

Just as people were trying to get in their last orders before 10:30, a fight broke out between two homeless dudes in the lobby area. Both reeked of alcohol and sweat; and were drunk as hell. Who the hell was that drunk at 10:30 in the morning? Marcus got them to settle down and separated by threatening to call the police and the promise of a complimentary cup of coffee. Three minutes later, Marcus delivered the coffee to the combatants, now seated on opposite sides of the restaurant.

At times it seemed like there were only three people, Marcus, Antoine and Trey - who was on the grill - holding it all together. Marcus did a little of everything during his shift: worked the front counter, worked the drive thru, packed orders, cleaned lobby tables, emptied garbage and broke up the fight. He was pretty sure that last part wasn't in the job description. And poor Antoine, he was running around like a chicken with his head cut off. Marcus wondered if he was starting to regret accepting the promotion. Ultimately though, he held it together.

Just as the lunch rush got into full swing and he was preparing to make his exit, since his shift ended at 12:00, Antoine approached.

"Can you stay until 2:00, Marcus?" he asked, "although I think we've got things under control, you know how hectic it can be at lunch. I'd like to have someone with experience around just in case." Although he really had no desire to stay and he had runs to make, he couldn't say no to Antoine. He was a good brotha. Marcus knew he had two kids at the house and his wife was finding it hard to hold down a job. God knows the promotion, the pay raise that came with it and being successful as a shift leader is just what

Antoine needed.

"Not a problem. Let me just take a quick break and get some fresh air." As he headed out the door, he thought to himself, *I'm really earning that $7.55 an hour today.* Two minutes later he was out back checking his text messages and responding to some clients. It was going to be a long afternoon with the extra time being put in here, but he should still be able to take care of all that he needed to this afternoon.

Thankfully, the last two hours proved to be uneventful. Each crew member pulled their weight and the customers were quite civil. Finishing up his shift, he grabbed his backpack, headed to the bathroom and changed into some fresh clothes. Instead of going straight home, he had a few deliveries to make on the way, and he didn't want to show up at client's homes in his McDonald's costume, smelling like a large order of fries or a chicken sandwich. Although he was a drug dealer, he didn't want to look like one, particularly when visiting the homes of his clients. Moreover, he had no desire to draw any unnecessary attention to himself. Changed and cleaned up, he very much looked like any of the Marquette students walking around the area.

Just as he was preparing to leave, Estelle walked in. Although she didn't stop by on a regular basis, it wasn't unusual to see her here. She did visit the restaurant occasionally. In fact, this is where he first met her. That was about 9 – 10 months ago. They struck up a conversation, and in passing, she mentioned that she suffered from some lower back pain. Laughing slightly, she said a friend had jokingly suggested, or at least Estelle thought she might be joking a little, she try marijuana. They both had heard it often relieved the pain. Marcus had nodded his head and agreed that he had heard the same thing.

Two or three visits later, she mentioned trying marijuana again. However, she had no idea how to go about getting some. Wisconsin wasn't like California or Oregon, where you could get medicinal marijuana with a doctor's prescription. Marcus casually noted, "I know someone. I might be able to get a little for you, see if it helps."

"Could you?" she asked. "Would you?" I wouldn't want you to get into any kind of trouble."

"It's not a problem," Marcus said. "You're not an undercover agent or something are you?"

"Ha!" she laughed. "Just call me secret agent grandma."

"I'm working tomorrow," Marcus said. "If you stop by about this time, I should have something for you." She did, and he did. That was how their relationship began.

As she was sitting down, Marcus told her to stay right there. He excused himself and was back in a few minutes with a fresh cup of coffee.

"Thank you, Marcus. A nice, hot cup of coffee is just what I needed." They exchanged some small talk for about 10 minutes and then Marcus excused himself.

"Well, I have to get going, Estelle. My work is never done."

"I know, dear," she said. "Take care and we'll talk soon."

"Yes we will," he said. With that, he made his exit.

Arriving at Corrine's, a podiatrist over at the Aurora Sinai Medical Center, he tapped on the door. She answered the door almost immediately. He dropped the two baggies on the table in the front entryway, she paid and they made some small talk.

"What do you think?" Corrine asked as she nodded slightly at the TV in the living room.

"They're debating how many states will legalize marijuana in the near future now that Washington State and Colorado have led the way. What do you think?"

"I think it's inevitable. When exactly? I have no idea. My guess is it'll be like a snowball that slowly gathers mass and momentum. Once it does get legalized in a few more states it'll happen pretty quickly. We'll see. In any event, I'll be done with this game within a year and I don't see it happening in Wisconsin before then."

"Well then, Marcus, I guess I will see you in a week or so."

"Sounds about right. Take care, Corrine."

Within four minutes he was headed out the door. He was always prompt in his arrivals, conducted business quickly, kept small talk to a minimum and made his exit.

As Redd had told him long ago, "You aren't there to hang out. It's not a social call and they ain't your friends. They're customers and you are there to provide a product. You want to walk in and be friendly and make conversation but also get to the business at hand and get out of there quickly." Of course, Estelle was the exception. His next three deliveries pretty much went the same way. Prompt arrival - based on the agreed time in the text messages - the transaction, some small talk and the exit. Just like Redd had preached.

Hopping on the bus, he was glad to get out of the cold. He thought he'd head home and grab a power nap. He was a little tired and Train was working. They would probably hook up later that night, see what they could get into. Stepping off the bus, he braced for the wave of cold air he knew would wash over him. And that it did. Making his way to the Square, he bounded up the steps and made his way into his apartment. Kicking off his shoes and throwing his backpack on the couch, he headed straight for the bedroom. Within three minutes he was out.

He was awakened an hour later by the sound of gunshots. It sounded like three. Two rapid pops, a short pause, and then one more. Four minutes later, the sound of sirens. Gunshots in this area were not unheard of; however, they weren't that common. As he lay there collecting his thoughts, wondering what prompted the gunshots, his phone vibrated incessantly on the nightstand. It was Train.

He was getting off work early and he would swing by in about an hour. Although he briefly considered laying back down for a minute, he sat up, stretched and headed for the kitchen. He was a little hungry so he figured he would cook up some ramen. Throwing in some leftover grilled chicken, an egg he scrambled quickly and cayenne pepper, to give it a little kick, he waited for it to finish cooking.

Just over an hour later, Train tapped on his door.

"What's goin' on, kid?" Train said, greeting him as he took off his coat. "Can I get a glass of water?"

"Not too much," said Marcus. "Just woke up a little bit ago. It was a crazy day at work today. Right before lunch, two homeless dudes squared off in the damn lobby. Both of them drunk as hell. Smelled like a damn brewery."

"Well, I guess that's one way to deal with this weather," Train offered. "Stay drunk and be completely oblivious to the cold." They both laughed as Marcus grabbed the water Train had asked for.

"Anything on the dude I described the other day?" Marcus inquired.

"In fact, yeah," Train said, "I reached out to a few people in the hood. Turns out his name is Drake, been in the area for a few months. Different people thought he came from either Chicago or Detroit. However, nobody seemed to really know what brought him here or what exactly his hustle is. So then I reached out to my cousin, Alesia. You remember her? I think you met her once over at Pere Marquette Park last year. She was a few years ahead of us in school."

"Yeah, I remember her," Marcus nodded affirmatively.

"Anyway, she ain't no detective or nothing, but she works for MPD as a records clerk. Been doin' that since last summer."

"She couldn't tell me a lot about him, but she did confirm he's from

Chicago, not Detroit, he used to dabble in dealing weed and he stays over on North 19th Street. Something else, and this is where it gets interesting, he didn't come alone."

"What do you mean? Does he have a wife and kids or something?"

"Nah. Turns out he traveled North with his cousin. A dude named Michael Simms. But apparently, he goes by the name Caine."

"What? as in Cain and Abel?" Marcus asked.

"Nope. Caine with an *e*, short for Cocaine," Train laughed. "I didn't know you was up on your Old Testament. Word is he moved a lot of coke in Chicago. Maybe they moved up here to just lay low for awhile. Who knows? As far as Alesia knows, from what she can tell, although suspected, he was never convicted of anything in Chicago and his only infraction here is a speeding ticket."

"Interesting," Marcus said, half under his breath as he laid back on the couch and closed his eyes for a minute. "The way his cousin, Drake, stared me down, I doubt if they are here on some sort of vacation or that they have decided to retire in Milwaukee. I don't know where drug dealers retire, but my guess is it ain't Wisconsin. It's gotta be something more. What? I don't know. I just don't know."

Glancing at the clock on the microwave, Marcus saw that it was almost 5:30 p.m., a good time to hit a couple of his spots and move some product. As Train excused himself to use the bathroom, Marcus grabbed his coat and 10 bags, slipping the weed into his inner pocket. When Train returned, he put on his coat and out the door they went. After about an hour, half that time spent at each spot, Marcus had moved all of his product.

"Nice," he said to Train as the last bag disappeared with Jorge, a fairly new customer, around the corner. Glancing at his watch, he noted that the timing was perfect. "My moms called earlier and wanted me to stop by for some dinner since I haven't been out that way in a while."

"Sounds good," Train said, "Renee gets off in about a half hour. If I hustle, I can be there when she gets off, take her out for a little dinner. Maybe hit KFC. That girl loves some extra crispy chicken and mashed potatoes with gravy. If I play my cards right, she might let me hit it tonight."

"Well good luck, my brotha. I hope you draw that inside straight." They both laughed as Train did an about face and took off for the shoe store where Renee worked.

Marcus broke out his phone and sent a quick text message: *to ma – be there in about 40 minutes.* Walking straight ahead, he headed for the bus stop.

He should be able to catch the bus within the next 15 minutes. Making the short walk to the corner he made the turn, side stepped a couple of kids and glanced down to zip up the jacket underneath his coat. He looked up just as he stepped right into Drake. The two were damn near eyeball to eyeball. Close enough to smell his cologne. Cool Water if he wasn't mistaken.

"What's goin' on, Man?" Drake said as he smiled. "Where you off to in such a hurry, Marcus?"

[5] THE MEET

Although he struggled to stay calm, Marcus' head was spinning. "Where did he come from? How did he know my name?" He didn't know the answers to those questions but he knew he had to keep his shit together. Be cool. Train was gone, he had caught a glimpse of the butt of a weapon stuffed into Drake's waistband - his catching a glimpse of the weapon was likely not a coincidence - and he had spotted the second brotha just over Drake's left shoulder, hangin' back a little, slowly surveying the area.

"Take a little trip?" Drake asked. Considering his options were somewhat limited, "Yeah," said Marcus. "We can take a little trip."

Motioning him over to a large, dark sedan, he instructed Marcus to get in the back seat. As darkness started to envelop the city, Marcus did as he was told. *It looks like I won't be making dinner tonight*, he thought to himself. *What have I gotten myself into?* Drake slid in next to him and his partner got behind the wheel. With his right hand in his waistband, Drake handed Marcus a dark bandana.

"Put it on and make sure it's tight." When Drake was satisfied that it was tight enough, he instructed the driver to drive.

Damn, Marcus thought to himself. The bandana was funky! It smelled like it had been dipped in a dirty toilet then hung out to dry. They drove for what seemed like 15 or 20 minutes and made quite a few turns. However, based on the inordinate amount of right hand turns, Marcus knew they were generally traveling in a circle. If he had to guess, he would say they were going to the place on North 19th Street. The place Alesia had told Train about. All that driving was probably just a crude attempt at disorienting him. With his vision impaired, Marcus' other senses went into overdrive. It was likely one or both of his would be kidnappers smoked. The smell hung in the air like a heavy fog. And although the radio was low, barely audible, it was tuned to V 107.1, the Jams. No other words were spoken until the car stopped, just as the last few notes of *Pills N Potions* by Nicki Minaj struggled to escape the car's woeful stock speakers.

"Get out," Drake instructed.

With the two of them on either side, they led him up some stairs. He counted as they led him up. Nine in all. Five in the first set, a short landing, and then four more. At the top, they stopped briefly on what felt like a neglected wooden deck. It had to be the porch. The sound of keys, a door opening and then they were inside. Finally the stinky bandana was removed. *Thank God for small favors*, he thought.

The house was dimly lit and it took a minute for his eyes to adjust following the removal of the bandana. Soon enough however, he was able to make out the general floor plan of the house. They were standing in the foyer. Living room straight ahead. Beyond that, a dining room with a hallway to the left. To the right, light spilled out of the room he assumed was the kitchen, the only room that appeared to be lit. The rest of the house, from what he could see, was cloaked in darkness.

Making their way through the living room and dining room, he glanced to the right. As he suspected, it was the kitchen, or at least what was once a kitchen. This one had been transformed into a packaging center. Though they moved past the room fairly quickly, Marcus glimpsed four women - half naked - working among what looked like cocaine, some weed, some blue crystals in baggies, boxes of baggies placed neatly on a shelf, multiple scales and a whole lot more. He couldn't see everything in the brief passing, but every indication was that this was more than just a couple guys looking to bank a few dollars from dealing a few drugs. This was something much larger. Much, much larger. While he had suspected the general nature of Drake's interest in him following his talk with Train, it was now becoming more clear what this 'visit' might be about.

They made their way down the hall toward the door at the end. Just short of the door, Drake guided him to a stop and tapped lightly on the door.

"Yeah," a voice called out from the other side.

"Watch him," Drake instructed his partner who had taken up a position behind Marcus' left shoulder, as he opened the room's door and let himself in.

An indecipherable, hushed conversation was all that Marcus could hear from the other side of the door. Moments later, the door opened and Drake waved Marcus in. He was helped along by the firm push to his left shoulder from behind. Marcus stepped in a few steps with his shadow close behind.

"That will be all. Thank you, Ricky," said the man seated in the chair.

"Yes, Sir," replied Ricky as he hastily retreated from the room, closing the door behind him.

So, we have Ricky and Drake; and this must be Caine, Marcus thought to himself. Of course, neither Drake nor Caine were aware that Marcus already knew who they were. He didn't yet know what they wanted with him, but he knew who they were. The room was dark. Darker than what was natural. Behind Caine's left shoulder the only window in the room had been covered with a black drape. No sunlight or moonlight was going to pierce that heavy cloth. The soft glow, from a small lamp in the corner, provided the only source of illumination.

Drake and Marcus just stood there and Caine sat in his chair. Even seated, it was clear that this was a big man. Marcus figured he was two to three inches taller than himself and easily 40 pounds heavier. This was a big man. As he took in the whole scene, the two images that came to his mind as he looked at Caine in his oversized chair were Robert DeNiro playing Luis Cyphre in that old movie *Angel Heart* and the Joffrey Baratheon character in *Game of Thrones*. Caine certainly had a high opinion of himself, sittin' in that big-ass chair.

"Please, have a seat," Caine offered as he indicated a small chair to Marcus' left. For a few moments, nothing else was said. *Perhaps they are waiting for me to ask why I'm here*, Marcus thought. Finally, "I'm Caine," the big man intoned, sounding a little bit like Barry White.

Marcus considered responding with, "I know," but thought better of it. Instead, he said, "Why don't you tell me why I was brought here?"

"Watch your tone, nigga," Drake advised him.

"As I'm sure you have seen, considering your brief pass by my packaging area, I deal drugs. However, what you might not appreciate is the breadth and scale of what I am planning with respect to distribution. Coke, crack, weed, heroine ... I plan to control it all, starting with weed. That's where you come in, Marcus. This is either a very lucky day for you or extremely unlucky."

"What do you mean?"

"I mean, I brought you here to give you a choice. Not all the dealers in the area will have a choice. Most will be strongly encouraged to cease their operations. Failure to do so will result ... let's just say it really will be in their best interest to find another vocation, a different line of work. However, those with common sense, a good work ethic and a demonstrable skill set, such as yourself, will be given the opportunity to join the team. As I said, it could be a very lucky day. However, if you choose not to work with me, like those that are not given a choice, you will need to cease your operations."

"And if I don't?"

Within his peripheral vision, all Marcus recalled seeing was a blur of movement on his right and then suddenly, there was the feel of cold metal against his right temple. Instinctively, he reached across with his left hand, placed his index and middle fingers on top of the barrel and gently pushed the gun down. Drake cocked the gun, a shell hit the floor and he started to raise the gun again.

"Whoa. Whoa!" Caine called out. "I don't think that will be necessary. It won't be necessary will it, Marcus?" As the adrenaline coursed through his body, Marcus glared straight ahead. "It won't be necessary will it, Marcus?"

"Nah, that won't be necessary. It's a lot to think about though. It is impossible for me to give you an answer right now," he managed through his tightened jaws and clenched teeth.

"Of course," Caine replied. "It is a lot to think about and I want you to have the time and an opportunity to make the right decision. I'm still getting a few things in place, so there is still a little time before I am ready to start things. Go live so to speak. One week, Marcus. You have one week to give me an answer." Reaching over and grabbing a small notepad off a side table, he scribbled something, ripped off the top sheet and handed it to Drake. Drake in turn gave the piece of paper to Marcus. "That's Drake's number. Don't lose it. If you have an epiphany and want to get started earlier, reach out." Without looking at it, Marcus stuffed into his pants pocket.

Behind him, Marcus heard the door open. Drake grabbed his right arm, stood him up, turned him around, and then they were walking.

"Oh, and one more thing," Caine called out before he had taken his second step. "I'm sure Marlon is hoping you will make the wise choice." And with that, that indirect threat hanging in the air, Drake marched him out the way they had come.

As they walked toward the front door, Marcus' mind was racing. Already, the encounter had a dreamlike quality. Later, the only thing he could remember about his exit were Ricky standing by the door – which appeared to be heavily reinforced – Drake handing him the stinky bandana, which he dutifully tied on, and the sound of Ricky opening the door. No dining room, no kitchen converted into a packaging area. Only Ricky, the bandana and the door.

Out on the porch, the air had cooled considerably. Down the steps the three of them went. Retracing their steps from earlier and getting in the car. What felt like about 20 minutes later, after another circuitous route, they dropped him in front of the Square. And just like that, the dark sedan was gone. Only the smell of an engine burning a little oil hung in the air. Feeling slightly nauseous he bent over, rested his hands on his knees and took a couple of deep breaths. After a minute or so he felt better and straightened up. *What have I gotten myself into?* Before he did anything else, he had to call his moms.

Reaching into his pocket, he pulled out his cell and saw that he had missed two calls from her. He tapped her picture. She picked up immediately.

"Hey, ma. Sorry I missed dinner. I wasn't feeling well and I fell asleep on the couch. How was dinner?"

"It was good. We had a little salad, some leftover mashed potatoes and I fried up some catfish that's been sitting in the refrigerator for a couple of days." You're not getting a cold or anything, are you, Baby?"

"No, ma. I'm good. Just a little tired. Work and this cold weather are beatin' me down. I'm gonna go lay back down and try to get a good night's sleep."

"Make sure you eat a little something and drink plenty of fluids."

"Will do, Ma. Love ya and I'll talk to you later."

"Marcus, before you go ..."

"Yeah, Ma?"

"Are you working tomorrow? If not, would you mind helping your father clean out some junk from the attic?"

"That's not a problem. I'm off during the day; I don't work until tomorrow night. How about I come by about 1:00 p.m., after lunch? I want to talk to Marlon anyway."

"About what?"

"Nothing much. You know. Brother stuff."

"Alright. We'll see you tomorrow."

"Love ya, ma. Good night."

One week, Marcus thought to himself. One week to make a decision. He didn't see working for Caine as a viable option. Not only did he not have a desire to work for someone else, he didn't want to be a part of anything that involved weapons and substantially more destructive drugs. However, he was not going to hit his college fund financial goal any time in the near future, certainly not in the next week. No doubt that Caine was quite serious, though. It was clear he had every intention of locking up distribution in this area. It would appear as if his options were limited. He was going to have to give this some serious thought.

Back in his apartment, Marcus headed straight for the kitchen. He was starving. Unfortunately, there wasn't much to choose from. It looked like his options were a bowl of Lucky Charms or some leftover lasagna. He decided on the lasagna. Something warm sounded more appetizing. While his plate of food warmed in the microwave, he headed to his bedroom, kicked off his shoes and changed into some sweatpants. Sitting on the edge of the bed, he had just started to give the encounter at Caine's a little more thought when he was snapped out of his reverie by the beeping microwave.

"I guess the lasagna is ready," he muttered to the empty space.

Grabbing his dinner, he headed into the living room and flipped on the television. Two hundred channels of shit to choose from. After a full minute of mindlessly tapping the 'channel up' button, he finally settled on CNBC which was doing an *American Greed* marathon. He loved Stacey Keach's intonation of "Scams, Scoundrels and Suckers." Although he had seen most of the episodes, he continued to be amazed at the number of people, who in many cases were smart enough to build substantial portfolios, yet weren't smart enough to avoid con artists promising, what appeared to be, obviously outsized returns. At the end of the day, it seemed to him that most of the 'victims' and perpetrators were two sides of the same greed coin. It was no wonder that avarice had made the list as one of the seven deadly sins. Halfway through the second episode he fell asleep.

Waking up at 2:30 in the morning, laying there on the couch with the television still on, he was momentarily disoriented. *American Greed* had been replaced by an infomercial for a magical expanding garden hose. *An interesting concept*, he thought. However, he didn't have a garden so he figured he didn't need one, magical or not. Dragging himself into an upright position, he reached for the remote, turned the television off and headed straight for his bed. Four hours later he was up again. *No alarm, no work today, ergo, no Groundhog Day* he thought to himself.

Considering he didn't have to work today, at McDonald's anyway, he thought he'd put in a longer run this morning, at least 3½ miles. Slipping on his shoes, some cold weather running gear, and grabbing his music, he stepped out his front door. Not as cold as the other morning, but still cool. He considered running over to 19th Street and seeing if he could identify Caine's place in the daylight.

He quickly dismissed the thought. He was as certain as he could be that's where he was last night. Moreover, what could he do there this morning? Nothing. Nothing could be accomplished by running past there. He needed to think this thing through; have a well thought out plan before engaging in any way with Caine. Using his better judgment, he turned and ran in the opposite direction.

Taking off at his customary leisurely pace, he settled into a nice rhythm and started to warm up a little. Making the turn at the two-mile point, which was about four songs from his playlist in his experience, he headed for home. No Carl today. In fact, not many people at all. There was very little traffic on the street this morning and quiet. Nice. He caught his second wind and let his mind drift a little as he increased the pace a little and held it all the way back to the Square. Feeling good this morning, he decided to do a long cool down. Instead of heading back to the apartment, he kept walking. Soon enough he found himself singing *All of Me* with John Legend.

Later that morning, Train dropped by and Marcus recounted the entire ordeal for him, starting with his unexpected encounter with Drake.

"After we parted, I stepped around the corner and there he was. Him and a partner. Dude named Rickey. Came out of nowhere." Marcus described getting in the sedan and the bandana that smelled like ass. "Then we drove for 15, maybe 20 minutes, but I'm pretty sure it was basically just in a circle and my bet is that we ended up at the house over on 19th Street, the one your cousin told you about. They didn't take off the bandana until we were inside so I can't be 100% certain."

"The inside of the house was crazy, man. I didn't realize until we were leaving, but the front door was heavily reinforced and they had converted the kitchen to a drug packaging center. Although we moved through the house, toward a back room fairly quickly, I saw four half-naked women packaging what looked like cocaine, some weed, and some type of blue crystal. In a back room is where I met this Caine. You ever see that old movie, *Angel Heart*?"

"Nah," said Train, shaking his head.

"You ever watch that show *Game of Thrones* on HBO?"

"Nope, but I know the show you're talking about though."

"Well, you ever see that big-ass chair, or throne I guess, that the crazy kid king sits in?"

"Yeah, I know what you're talking about."

"Well, that's what Caine's chair looked like. Not in appearance necessarily, but sheer size. And it had to be big, 'cause he's a big brotha, who sounded a lot like Barry White."

"Barry White?"

"Yep."

Train started humming *Your Sweetness is My Weakness*. "Please," Marcus begged, "just don't start singing." Marcus had heard what Train called singing and it wasn't music to his ears. He imagined that Train doing his best Barry White imitation, or any Barry White imitation, his best or worst, would be quite painful.

"Once I was seated, Caine laid it all out. He told me that he had brought me there to give me a choice. "A choice? What kind of choice?"

"According to Caine, not all the dealers in the area would have a choice. Most would be strongly encouraged to cease their operations, move on to other work. The only reason I was being given a choice was because I possessed some common sense and a demonstrable skill set. Apparently, they've been watching a lot of dealers in the area, sizing us all up. The bottom line is that he plans to control all distribution in this area, not just weed. He talked about an operation of significant breadth and scale. He plans on controlling it all - coke, crack, weed, meth, heroin - everything. At one point, Drake even pulled a gun on me to demonstrate how serious they were."

"Damn!" Train said, "sounds like they do mean business.

"One week. That is how much time he is giving me to 'join the team' as he put it. But that is not the worst part."

"What else could there be after wearing that funky-ass bandana and having a gun pulled on you?"

"As I was leaving, he dropped Marlon's name. "I'm sure Marlon is hoping you will make the wise choice,' he said."

"What the fuck!?" exclaimed Train. "Your brother? This dude ain't some amateur. He has done more than just check out your activities in the area. He's researched your family. Damn!"

"After that, we went through the same routine, in reverse, to leave. Bandana, back into the car, driving around for about 15 minutes or so and then they dropped me off in front of the Square. One week to make a decision."

"It seems to me you don't really have any options," Train suggested.

"Not many anyway. I don't see working for Caine as a viable option. I don't have a desire to work for someone else and I definitely don't want to be a part of anything that involves weapons or shit like heroin and cocaine. However, I'm not going to hit my financial goals any time in the near future, certainly not in the next week. I have got to figure out a way to stay out of his crosshairs, conduct my business and keep making my money."

[6] WORK

There wasn't a lot of time to figure out what he was going to do. One week. The only thing he knew for certain was that he was not going to deal for Caine. He just needed to figure out how to decline 'his offer' and find a way to continue servicing his clients to ensure his income stream was not negatively impacted. Although a week wasn't a lot of time, he definitely did not want to be rash in his decision-making.

He figured the best approach was to do nothing today. Just run through some various scenarios in his head and see if he could generate some good ideas. He would treat today just like any other day when he had a late shift at Mickey D's. He needed to get by the bank sometime today and he had to get over to his parents by 1:00 p.m. Easiest thing to do would be to hit the bank this morning, make a small deposit, and then grab some lunch on the way to his parent's place. Grabbing his backpack, he packed it with his McDonald's gear and headed out.

The bank was considerably busier than the last time he was there. Tracy was working, but he wasn't sure he would be able to time it so that she would wait on him. He'd give a shot though. As he approached the front of the line, he offered an older gentlemen his spot when it looked like the teller to Tracy's left would finish her current transaction first.

"Thank you, young man."

"You're welcome, Sir." As the teller adjacent to Tracy finished, he mumbled, "Perfect."

"Next guest in line, please," she called out. The gentlemen obliged and headed that way.

Looking up, Tracy recognized him, and if he wasn't mistaken, there was the faintest of smiles. Approaching the counter, he gave her his customary smile and salutation.

"How are you this fine morning, Ms. Tracy?"

"I'm well. And yourself Mr. Williams?"

"No complaints."

"Making a deposit in your savings account this morning?" she asked.

He maintained his emergency fund in the savings account. This deposit would be into his regular checking account.

"No, Ma'am. The checking account," he said as he slid the deposit slip toward her.

Sensing an opening, he asked, "When are you going to let me take you

41

out to dinner?"

Without missing a beat, she replied, "As soon as you ask, probably." Taken aback for a minute, but just a minute, Marcus gathered his composure.

"Well let's see, I'm working tonight and tomorrow, how about Friday night?"

"That's fine."

"Can I get your ..." Looking down, he saw that she had written down her number on the receipt she had just slid his way.

"Have a good day, Mr. Williams. Next guest in line, please."

Did that really just happen? he wondered. While he was absolutely thrilled with what just happened, he had not imagined it when he walked into the bank six minutes ago. What a difference six minutes can make. If he would have been in one of those old movies he would have jumped and clicked his heels as he was walking out. *Yep, today was a good day.*

Considering the options that were nearby, and his desire to reduce the amount of fast-food he ate, he decided to just wait until he got to his parent's house to eat. No matter what his moms made he knew it was going to be good. Making his way over to the MCTS bus stop, he approached the bench and started to have a seat. The gum and dark gray, unidentifiable matter covering half the bench convinced him he might be better off standing. Hopefully the bus would be here soon. Looking down the street for the bus, anticipating its arrival, he saw a homeless dude, with three suitcases and two small bags, approaching the stop. The old timer was struggling a little bit with all his gear, so Marcus offered a hand.

"Can I give you a hand, Sir?"

"You most certainly can, young man. Thank you." No sooner had they finished getting him squared away the bus appeared, seemingly out of nowhere. Opening the door, the bus driver smiled and waited patiently as they dragged the suitcases and bags on board. Most of the other passengers weren't as patient, nor did any of 'em offer to help.

After a few minutes they were on their way. Or so they thought. At the very next stop, the old dude disembarked, and they went through the same routine in reverse. Marcus couldn't help but chuckle to himself. *I'll be damned*, he thought. *All that for a 38 second ride to the next stop.* Without a moment's hesitation, he helped the dude and his bags off. Again, no one else offered any assistance and if they were slightly annoyed before, they were really annoyed now! Not the bus driver though. He sat, waited patiently, and smiled the entire time. Public service at its finest.

Making the change to a new line four stops later, Marcus' timing was perfect. He only had a three minute wait until the bus came. Hopping on board, he walked to the back row and plopped down. He had a 15 minute ride in front of him, so he just wanted to sit back and relax a little. *Where should I take Tracy for dinner?* he thought. If she liked sushi, he was thinking Umami Moto over on North Milwaukee Street. He had heard that it was excellent. If she didn't do sushi, maybe a good steakhouse. Wherever they went, he'd have to borrow Train's car. It wasn't the fanciest car and it didn't run great, particularly in cold weather, but it beat the hell out of walking.

Arriving at his parent's house, he let himself in.

"Hey, Ma," he called out.

"I'm in the kitchen, Marcus." He walked in and had a seat.

"How you feeling today?" she asked. It took him a half second to figure out why she was asking.

"Not too bad. A lot better than yesterday. Where's Pops?"

"He should be back soon. He just ran to the store to pick up some trash bags and cleaning supplies. Can I get you something to eat, Baby?"

"Yes, Ma'am. What are my options?"

"Got a little of the catfish left over. That or I could make you a ham and cheese sandwich."

"The sandwich sounds good. What time does Marlon get home from school?"

"Usually about 2:45." Just then, he heard the front door open and a moment later, his father appeared in the kitchen.

"How ya doing today, Pop?"

"I'm well, son. Yourself?"

"Not too bad. I got a good night sleep and I'm ready to tackle that attic. Just as soon as your wife feeds me." They both laughed as his father headed to their bedroom to get changed. When he was finished with his sandwich, Marcus stepped out on the porch to get some fresh air ... and to reply to his text messages, before heading up to the attic.

It had been years since he had been in the attic. It was a lot worse than he remembered but not as bad as he imagined it might be. While there was plenty of old stuff, most not worth keeping from what he could tell, there seemed to be more papers – and dust – than anything else. They worked through the mess fairly quickly. His father looking through boxes of paperwork, determining what could be kept and what could be tossed, and Marcus dragging stuff downstairs and separating into two distinct piles. Stuff that was worth carting over to the Goodwill and stuff destined for the trash. Two and a half hours later they were finished. All the trash separated and the floor swept and mopped.

Sitting down in the living room watching TV, and growing a little tired, Marcus was just about to leave when Marlon finally showed up, 45 minutes after he was expected. Apparently there was a problem with bus, holding him up for awhile.

"What's going on, young brother?"

"You know, just this school thing. It isn't too bad." A sophomore, Marlon still had a couple years of high school left. Following him to his room, Marcus asked, "How them grades looking?"

"You're starting to sound like Pops."

"Ouch," Marcus said as he feigned getting shot. "Like, Pops? Wow. That hurt."

"Notice anything out of the ordinary lately?"

"What do you mean out of the ordinary?" Marlon asked as a quizzical look spread across his face. Marcus gave him the heavily sanitized version of his meeting with Caine, leaving out details such as the gun and the quantity and types of drugs involved; and then he gave the description of Drake.

"Dark-skinned, a little shorter than me, kinda stocky and bald with a goatee. Seen anybody new hangin' around school? Anybody that fits that description?"

"Nah, man," Marlon assured him.

"Well, be observant and let me know if you see anything, and I mean anything, out of the ordinary."

"Yeah, will do. Staying for dinner?"

"Nope, not tonight, young man. Got a shift at work. As a matter of fact, I need to go change. Leaving his brother's room, he headed back to the living room, grabbed his backpack, stepped into the bathroom and quickly changed.

Back down in the kitchen, he spoke with his parents for a few minutes before getting ready to go.

"Thanks for the help today, Marcus."

"You're welcome. It looks a lot better up there." Giving his moms a hug and a kiss on his way out, she whispered, "Thank you, Baby. It's nice to see you and your father working together."

"Not a problem," he whispered back. "I'll talk to you guys later," he said as pulled the front door closed behind him.

Headphones on, top button buttoned, collar up and he was off to the bus stop. *Hopefully there won't be any more patrons with multiple suitcases taking one block trips on the MCTS*, he laughed to himself. Fast forwarding through the first four songs that popped up on random play, he decided to let *Black*

Widow by Iggy Azalea play. Turning up the volume a little, he settled into a seat near the back of the bus.

No bus drama on this late afternoon. Everything couldn't have been more normal. No vagabonds and the bus made its journey, at least during the time Marcus was on board, without anything crazy happening. Even got him to work a few minutes earlier than expected. Same story at work. Vanessa was back and seemingly none the worse for the wear after her bout with illness. A short four hour shift and he was on his way home.

Just like everything else that night, the bus ride home was uneventful. Getting off the bus, he made the short walk to the Square. Hearing a slight noise to his right rear, he yanked off his headphones and turned quickly. Nothing. Just the wind maybe? Jeez, he really was getting paranoid. Heading for the stairs he caught sight of the rear of a dark sedan just as it turned the corner and was out of sight. Paranoia? Maybe. Probably didn't matter anyway. Even if it was Drake, probably nothing to worry about. What was he going to report back to Caine? That Marcus rode the bus a lot today and worked? Nothing new or exciting there. He figured there was nothing to worry about for now. He had six days. Six days before he had to render his decision.

Startled awake by the blare of his alarm clock, Marcus rolled over and hit the off button. Just what he needed. A good night sleep. Surprisingly, considering the recent drama with Drake and Caine, he just had the best night sleep in as long as he could remember. It had been awhile since he had such a lucid, vivid dream. In his dream he was flying but had trouble staying aloft; he couldn't get enough lift to make his way past trees or over power lines. He'd have to go online and get an interpretation of the dream.

Wiping the sleep from his eyes, he sat up and let his feet fall to the floor. Sitting there on the edge of the bed, he stretched out for a few minutes before dropping to the floor for some push-ups and sit-ups. One hundred and fifty each, six sets of twenty-five, should do it. Always a fabulous way to start the day.

Making his way toward the kitchen, he grabbed the remote off the coffee table and turned on the television, going directly to CNBC. As was the case most mornings, the station would serve as adequate background noise while he made his breakfast and got ready for work. On the TV, a market strategist was laying out his vision of where the market was headed:

"As the Fed ends its massive bond-buying program, a policy that has been blamed for fuelling rising stock prices over the past few years, I suspect stocks will see a 20 percent correction, likely at the start of the new year. As the U.S. central bank begins to raise interest rates and investors feel the effects of a world without cheap money, watch out."

Instead of his normal smoothie for breakfast, he opted for a couple of scrambled eggs, half a grapefruit and his coffee. Following a long, leisurely shower, he sat down at the computer and opened up the financial spreadsheet he maintained. Listening to the TV in the background, a bond fund manager was talking about yields:

> "It will be interesting to see if the 10-year yield gets below 2.35 percent. If that's the case I do think we're going to 2.20. U.S. Treasury yields are being dragged down by moves in the European bond market. At this point it's a momentum trade. People are looking for safety and obviously the Treasury bond market looks relatively attractive versus other bond markets. Moreover, I believe the Fed's zero interest rate policy will be with us longer than most think."

While he was familiar with bonds and how they worked in general, they were one of the areas of investing he wanted to gain more knowledge of. *Yep, I will have to do that*, he thought as he added it to his mental 'to do' checklist.

The spreadsheet was how, and where, he tracked all his expenses, the balances of his savings and investment accounts; basically, all of his finance related information and goals. He updated it as necessary, such as the recent deposit into his emergency fund, and conducted a detailed quarterly analysis to verify progress and make adjustments as necessary. While sitting at the computer, he quickly searched for 'interpreting flying dreams.' *Interesting*, he thought.

According to a couple sites he came across, having difficulties staying in flight indicated a lack of power in controlling your own circumstances; trouble staying on a set course. The obstacles encountered in flight symbolize something or someone who is standing in your way in your waking life. The recommendation was to identify what or who is trying to prevent you from moving forward. *Well I know who is trying to prevent me from moving ahead. I know the individuals responsible for fucking up my flight plan.* With the spreadsheet updated and looking good; and his dream interpreted he checked the plants - all good - grabbed his backpack and was out the door.

Vanessa put him on the front counter, letting him know as soon as he walked in.

"You're on the counter with, Barb." As he passed her by, she lowered her voice. "I know she can be slow, so I wanted to pair her with somebody that knows what the hell they're doing."

"Not a problem. I got this," he replied.

Contrary to the popular urban myth, people would be happy to know that in all his time working at McDonald's he had never seen anybody put anything in the food. While they might bitch about a customer that returned something, fouling the guest's food was out of bounds. Way out of bounds! Generally, the bitching about customers was pretty trivial. Sometimes valid, sometimes not. An invalid bitch? Like today, a couple crewmembers were complaining about customers that ordered Big Breakfasts and Happy Meals because they took too long to make.

A valid bitch? Customers that make their job harder, simply because they can, or because they are self-centered fools. Today was a prime example of the latter. With a long line at the counter, and Barb only managing one transaction to his every two, he spotted a 4 or 5 year old girl playing with the soda fountain; and of course, her mother was completely oblivious, pounding out what appeared to be a series of long text messages. The kid had held the lemonade handle in the down position, filling her cup and beyond.

He tried to get the mom's attention between helping guests, to no avail. Finally, Jackson, who was in the lobby cleaning tables and emptying trash, saw what was going on. But hell, by the time he got over there, the kid had drained the lemonade. Had to be a gallon or more of lemonade on the lobby floor. The mother, who had finally managed to pay attention to her child, could only offer a "Sorry," as Jackson rolled his eyes and hustled to the closet for a mop and bucket. Unbelievably, she went right back to her phone, completely engrossed with the device and her electronic conversation.

Just as he was about to take a break he noticed Maria had just headed out for hers. He didn't really feel like engaging in small talk with her today. Plus, he had a ton of business to attend to when he did take his break. At his last count, he had 12 text messages. He assumed most of those were delivery related. He would wait a few to take his break. "After your next guest, Barb, go ahead and take your break. I'll let you grab yours first."

"Thanks, Marcus. I could use a break."

Well, the need certainly isn't a result of working too hard or too fast, Marcus thought to himself.

Fifteen minutes later, five minutes beyond the allotted time, Barb strolled back in and Marcus let Vanessa know that he was going to take his break. She directed Jess, a capable, experienced crewmember, to come to the front and work with Barb. God knew she couldn't handle the counter by herself. When Jess was ready to go, Marcus stopped by the men's room and washed his hands before heading outside. His hands felt grimy and smelled like copper after handling what seemed liked 200 cash transactions. As he made his way to the area our back he reveled in the fresh air. Although cold, the air felt good. He needed the break.

Just as he had come out, Brian, who was working the grill, was heading back in.

"How ya doing today, Brian?" Marcus asked.

"I'm good. You know how it is. Just trying to get by. Been lookin' for another job."

"Something else or in addition to this one?"

"In addition to. Shoot, I can't afford to have just one job. But it's hard to keep another job when the schedules here vary week to week. I talked to Vanessa about getting some fixed hours. She said she would see what she could do. We'll see."

"I hear ya, man. Hard to get a second job when the hours are always changing and the one job ain't enough to pay bills. People get stuck. They say that fast-food jobs are mostly for teenagers and people in transition, but that ain't what I see. I see a whole lot of old folks, 40 and older, working fast-food for a long time and it's their only source of income. Hell, look around here. You got John, Klarissa, Melba ..."

"What's her name, Helen," Brian added.

"Yep, Helen too. It's crazy man. This economy and the job situation is just plain crazy."

"Yep, I don't want to be 40 and still working here. Anyway, I better get back in to make sure I hold on to this one for now. I don't want Vanessa losing her mind if I'm a few minutes late comin' back in."

Marcus knew that the only way to have any chance of making it out here was to get an education and develop a plan for making, and saving, your money. Otherwise it's a paycheck to paycheck existence in low-wage jobs. *Living paycheck to paycheck. Not for me,* he thought. Pulling out his phone, he started going through his messages. Just as he thought, they were mostly delivery related. Methodically he went through them one at a time, setting up delivery times. A couple of minutes later, he started getting confirmations. So far, it looked like he was going to have at least four today and at least three tomorrow morning. He wanted to make sure everybody was taken care of tonight or tomorrow morning. He would be busy tomorrow night.

Just as he was heading back in, one of the new guys, Elroy, who had just got off the training program, was walking out.

"How ya doing, Elroy?"

"I'm good, Marcus. Might be doin' a little better if you squared me away."

Playing dumb, Marcus asked, "What do you mean?"

"You know. I was hoping you could square me away with a bag of weed."

"Not me, man. I used to deal, but not anymore. Too crazy a life. You must have got some bad information. Who suggested you come see me?"

"Just kind of heard it through the grapevine."

"Maybe from Marvin Gaye or somebody?" Marcus offered.

"Who?"

"Enjoy your break and be on time comin' back in, Marcus suggested. You just started and you don't want to get on Vanessa's bad side."

Interesting, I wonder where that came from? Marcus thought. That was the first time somebody had ever approached him at work. He made a point not to mix McDonald's with his side hustle. That was asking for trouble. The exceptions were Maria and Pete whom he had been dealing to before he started here. His relationship with them went back to before his time at McDonald's. Plus, they knew better than to send business to him in that way. Plus that fool didn't know Marvin Gaye? That was reason enough not to deal with him. *Very interesting indeed*, he thought. Sliding his phone back into his pocket, he headed back inside. Just another couple hours and this shift would be done, in the books.

The rest of his shift went pretty smoothly and the two hours sailed by. Barb even seemed to get into a nice rhythm toward the end. She was still slower than most, but for her, the times for each transaction were much better. Stepping through the door after clocking out and changing, Marcus threw his headphones on his head and his back pack over his shoulder, checked his phone - nothing new - and headed for the bus stop. He ended up needing to make five deliveries this afternoon. He would have to hustle to make his times.

Thankfully, Marcus got through the first four deliveries without any issues. He was on time, everybody was at home, small talk was had and payments were made. All good. He saved the last visit for Franklin. Next to Estelle, he was probably the client with whom Marcus had established the friendliest relationship.

Approaching Franklin's Duplex, Marcus fired off a quick text message: *to Train – need to borrow your car tomorrow night if possible.* Almost immediately, he received a text response: *from Train – not a problem drop off about 5:00.* His attention distracted, Marcus was a little startled when Franklin approached him from behind.

"Hey, how ya doing, Marcus? Looks like I got here just in time. Had to run back to the office for a minute." Reaching his door, Franklin opened up and they stepped in.

Dressed in his scrubs, Franklin looked every bit a doctor. However, he was actually a nurse. Marcus had read somewhere that only about 7% of nurses in the U.S. are males. He imagined Franklin caught flak from people that have a fixed image of what a nurse looks like. But Franklin had it going on. He was actually nearly finished with his doctoral in nursing program. Marcus had never heard of such a thing until introduced to Franklin via Corrine. A doctor of nursing. Who knew?

After a little chit chat - the weather, his upcoming finals and the state of the economy - Marcus reached into his backpack and pulled out a couple of baggies at the same time Franklin started to hand him the money. Making their exchange, Franklin asked, "You wanna roll one before you go?"

"Nah, I appreciate it, man, but you know I don't smoke."

"So you always say."

"And you always ask. Just never something that held my interest. Well, I gotta go, Franklin. Take care and we'll talk soon." With that he was out the door and headed back to the Square. From here it was just as easy to walk. Pulling his cap out of his pocket, he slipped it on his head, hunched his shoulders, buried his hands in his pockets and started his walk.

[7] DELIVERIES

Waking before the alarm clock went off, Marcus reached over and shut it off before it did. Sitting up and stretching for a minute, he shook off the last vestiges of sleep and headed for the kitchen to get a drink of water. Standing in his kitchen, he reviewed his plans for the day in his head. A nice long workout this morning, a little breakfast, deliveries later and dinner with Tracy tonight. Finishing up his water, he headed to the living room and docked his iPhone to his stereo. Scrolling to his 'workout' playlist, he turned the volume up; just a little, he didn't want to be a rude neighbor. A little music while he worked out would be good. He decided to work chest and triceps this morning. Moments later, *Lazy Love* by Ne-Yo filled the quiet space.

Starting with chest, he grabbed the only dumbbells he had, 30 pounders, laid down on the floor and commenced to doing some flys, 12 repetitions. He followed those up with flex and squeezes – squeezing the chest muscles for 10 seconds and holding – and finished with close grip pushups, 10 repetitions. Cycling through those four exercises, he repeated the routine four times.

Moving on to triceps, he grabbed one of the 30 pound dumbbells and started with overhead extensions, 12 repetitions each arm. He followed those with flex and squeezes – squeezing the triceps for 10 seconds and holding – and finished by walking over to a chair in the kitchen, using it to do chair dips, 10 repetitions. Like with his chest routine, he cycled through these three exercises four times. As his iPhone cycled through his playlist, he finished up by cooling down with a good stretch and some deep breaths.

"Cereal or a smoothie this morning?" Marcus asked the empty room. Opening the fridge, his answer was made easier as it turned out he had run out of milk and eating the cereal dry was not an option. That worked out well since he happened to have lots of fruit around and some kale he wanted to use up. Yep, you have to love those green, leafy vegetables. A little ice, some almond soy, low-fat yogurt, a couple of apples and the kale and he was good to go. After a 30-second blend he poured the velvety smooth drink into a tall glass, grabbed a straw and headed for the living room.

Turning off the stereo and turning on the TV, he plopped down on the couch. He started to tune the TV to Bloomberg TV and then changed his mind. Instead, he switched the TV to the HDMI 1 input, fired up his Apple

TV and opened up the Netflix app. He figured he would watch the second half of the documentary he had started about a week ago, *Inequality for All.* Estelle had recommended the film and it was pretty interesting so far.

The film follows Robert Reich, a former U.S. Labor Secretary under President Bill Clinton, as he tries to raise awareness of the country's widening economic gap. He notes that we are currently in the biggest economic slump since the Great Depression. His suggestion is that a significant factor for this current economic state is because – just like the 1920s – so much of the nation's income and wealth are going to the top and the shrinking middle class does not have the purchasing power to keep the economy going.

Most interesting to Marcus, Reich notes that Americans are stressed, angry, and frustrated. No doubt, he had seen plenty of that. From the Tea Party, to the short lived Occupy movement, to the recent minimum wage protests by fast-food workers, people were definitely pissed off. It seemed like those that have jobs are working harder, working longer, suffering under the weight of debt and not getting ahead. Resuming the film, Reich was talking about worker's rights:

> "If workers don't have power, if they don't have a
> voice, their wages and benefits start eroding ... "

Pausing the documentary, he got up, and headed back to the kitchen where he placed his smoothie glass in the sink and made himself a cup of coffee. Had to have his java every morning! Back in the front of the TV, he watched the rest of the documentary while he enjoyed his coffee.

After late-night exchanges of text messages, it looked like he was going to have to make two more deliveries today, making it a total of six. He wanted to be finished by 4:00 p.m., which meant that he should probably head out soon. Turning off the TV and hopping up off the couch, he dropped his coffee mug off in the kitchen before heading back to his bedroom to grab a shower.

Forty-five minutes later, Marcus was out the door with his backpack slung over his shoulder. His first delivery was within walking distance, about a mile away. Twenty minutes later, he was buzzed into a recently renovated ground-floor apartment and greeted by Rhonda, a middle-age blond woman. A newer customer, Rhonda looked pretty stylish in her dark cashmere sweater and form fitting jeans.

The visit was short. Marcus produced the two bags requested by Rhonda. She paid immediately and offered a glass of water.

"No thank you. I appreciate it though. I have to get going. Make my rounds and get back home." With that, he was out the door and on to the next client.

Outside his preferred walking distance, Marcus headed to the bus stop for transportation to his next appointment. When he arrived, Janice, a graduate student at Marquette - and one of the few black clients that made use of his delivery service - anxiously awaited by the door.

"Ah, right on time. I'm so glad. I'm already running late." That wasn't a problem for Marcus. Although they sometimes did the chit chat thing for a minute, today he was in a hurry himself. Better to wrap up the deal quickly and be on his way, which is exactly what he did. Very quickly, they thanked each other and he was gone.

In a case of sublime planning and fortunate timing, the next appointment was right around the corner. Literally only a two-minute walk away. Reaching Harold's door, Marcus tapped lightly. Nothing. Waiting a minute or so, he knocked again, a little bit harder. Still nothing. Giving it one final knock, Marcus had started to leave when Harold finally opened up.

"I was just about to leave, man."

"Sorry, I was in the bathroom. I tried to pinch it off and get to the door as soon as I heard you."

Whoa! A little TMI, Marcus thought as he stepped through the door. As always, Harold was good for three bags. Immediately, he began tearing up the sticky weed and shoving it into a glass bong. Shoving the bong toward Marcus, "Smoke?"

"Thanks, but no thanks. I don't smoke, man."

"Really? Cool."

"Alright, Harold. I have to go. Take care and we'll be in touch soon, I'm sure." *And even if I did smoke, I'm pretty sure I wouldn't be interested after the comment about pinching it off and rushing to the door*, Marcus thought to himself.

Unlike two nights ago, when he caught just a glimpse of the rear of the sedan as it was turning the corner and wasn't sure if it was Drake or not, that wasn't the case now. Down the street, about a block away, Drake sat in the parked sedan. No doubt that he was being followed. Perhaps not all the time, but they were certainly keeping any eye on his movements. Still a few days to go before a decision had to be made, but clearly, a plan had to be formulated soon. Ignoring the sedan, he went on about his way. The next stop required him to take the bus, so he headed that way. Checking his watch, if he wasn't mistaken, he had about nine minutes until the next bus was scheduled to arrive.

The next two deliveries, Shawn and Jordan, were drama free. Both were home and paid quickly. Just what Marcus was hoping for. And as far as he could tell, no more Drake. Perhaps he was tired of following him today? While he wasn't worried about being followed himself, he was definitely concerned about what his side hustle, and the introduction of Drake and Caine into his life, might mean for his family and any potential relationship with Tracy.

He had already given some thought to how to address what he did on the side if it came up. Actually, it was more a case of when it came up. If they ended up spending any time together, it would definitely come up. As of right now, he didn't have a good idea of how he would handle that conversation. He guessed he would just deal with it if, when, the time came.

The last stop was Charles. Probably the most mysterious of all of Marcus' clients. While his dress and speech suggested he was a young professional, he had never revealed exactly what he did or where he did it. He played it pretty close to the vest. That was fine with Marcus. He could appreciate it if someone wasn't interested in sharing a lot of information about themselves. He was fine with keeping the relationship strictly about business. Oddly enough, Charles chose this day to be a Chatty Cathy. Or maybe Chatty Charlie was more accurate.

"How's the weather out there today? I haven't been out yet."
"Not too bad," Marcus said, "the occasional gust of wind makes it seem a little colder than it really is. The old wind chill factor. They say there is a slight chance of snow later. No work for you today?"
"No. Although I feel better now, I woke up with a headache and a little nausea. Figured I would take a sick day"
"Maybe you're pregnant," Marcus offered.
"Yeah, maybe that's it," Charles said, laughing.
They talked a little about the upcoming Packers game that weekend and the ongoing community renovation initiatives. They agreed that things in Avenues West were looking better, slowly but surely.
"Well, I have to go, Charles. Take care and we'll talk soon."
"Sounds good. Take care and thanks for the product, Marcus."

Back out in the elements, Marcus took a quick look around. No obvious sign of Drake. Now that he thought about it, he didn't feel that great himself. Checking the time, it was just shy of 2:00 p.m. He had about three hours before Train would be bringing the car by. If he hustled home, he could grab a two-hour power nap. He wanted to be in top form for his date tonight. With that, he hustled to the bus stop. Must of have been his lucky day. Within a minute of arriving at the stop, he looked up and there was the bus, barreling toward the stop. Nice.

[8] THE DATE

Just before 5:00 p.m. the sound of his phone vibrating on the nightstand woke him from his deep slumber. It was Train. He would be there in about 15 minutes. Perfect. Sitting up, he took a few deep breaths to clear the cobwebs and assess how he felt. Did the nap do the trick? Oh yeah. He felt a lot better. He was ready for the night. It seemed like no sooner had he gotten up and started moving around that Train was tapping on his door.

"Hey there, Kid. I appreciate you letting me use the car tonight."

"Don't worry about it. Hell, I need somebody to put some gas in the tank. You'll be doing me a favor."

"I should have known you had an angle." They shared a laugh as they moved into the living room, where Marcus turned on the TV.

"Get you some water or something? Some juice maybe?"

"No, Man. I'm good. So what's going on? Stay busy today?"

"Yep. Made a bunch of deliveries earlier then came home and laid down for a minute. Didn't feel quite 100%."

Marcus then gave Train a rundown of the day, particularly the spotting of Drake.

"I had about six deliveries today. Started with a new customer, Rhonda. Then I stopped in to see Janice. I told you about her, right? The sista that's a grad student at Marquette?"

"Yeah, you mentioned her before."

"After Janice I went to see that fool, Harold. Kind of a strange cat. He invited me to stay to smoke a bowl. Of course I declined and just tried to keep the convo brief and get out of there. When I left, I saw Drake sitting in that sedan, parked down the street. I'm not sure what they hope to accomplish by following me, but it's clear Caine will be looking for my response in a few days."

"I know you said you weren't going to work for him. So what are you going to do?"

"I still don't know yet. Not exactly. Still knocking some ideas around in my head."

"Did you see Drake any more today or just that one time?"

"Just that one time. I had three more deliveries after that, but no Drake. Been here since."

"Well, my man, I'm gonna go and let you get ready."

"You want me to drop you off someplace?" asked Marcus. I've got plenty of time to get you to Renee's, or anywhere else, and still get ready."

"I'm good. Go ahead and get ready. I'm just gonna take the bus over to Renee's."

"Let me drop you off, Train."

"No, it's alright. Go ahead and get ready. I want to make sure you have plenty of time to stop and get some gas. The 91 octane, premium shit. None of that cheap, 84 octane stuff."

"Should I get a receipt just to verify which grade of gasoline I purchase?"

"Would you mind?"

"Get out of here," Marcus said as they both laughed all the way to the door. "I do appreciate it, Train."

"Not a problem. Give me a call tomorrow and let me know how it went."

"Will do," said Marcus.

After Train left, Marcus headed straight to the bathroom to start getting ready. Jumping in the shower, he broke out his favorite smell good body wash and new loofah body scrub. Rub-a-dub-dub! Yes, Sir. It was going to be a good night. Finishing up the shower, he wrapped a towel around his waist and ran out to the stereo, attached his iPhone and selected random play. "Yep, a little music while I get ready," he sang out to the room. A little *Sailin' Away* from Mr. Anthony Hamilton. *Now that's a nice start.*

Back in his bedroom, Marcus slipped on a pair of jeans, a dark crew cut sweater and his black Doc Martens, his favorite shoes. A splash of Calvin Klein's Eternity for Men, a gift from his parents last Christmas, completed the transformation. Checking himself out in the mirror, he felt like he was good to go. "Damn, you are good looking young man," he said to the man in the mirror. Picking up his phone, he sent a message: *to Tracy – be there in 15 minutes.* Although he didn't expect her to respond immediately, he got a little nervous when six minutes later she had not replied.

"Had she forgot? Was she blowing him off? Should he go ahead and head over there? If he was going to make it by the time he said, he should have left a few minutes ago. But then again, he hated to leave without some type of confirmation that she was ready, or would in fact, be there. He was considering sending another text but that might come across as desperate or even worse, maybe a little creepy. Just as all those thoughts and questions ran through his head, he heard that familiar tone of a text message: *from Train - have fun tonight kid.* Twenty seconds later, another text message: *from Tracy – sounds good just got off the phone with my mom.* And with that, he grabbed his wallet and Train's car keys and was out the door.

Although he had spoken to her on a number of occasions and this wasn't a blind date or something, he was nervous. More nervous than he should have been. *Relax, Marcus*, he thought to himself. The last thing he wanted to do was to start sweating and get some big-ass sweat stains in his arm pits. Stopping in front of her house, he broke out a piece of gum. Had to make sure the breath was fresh. He couldn't risk it smelling like that bandana. Jumping out of the car, he made his way to the front door. Almost immediately, it opened. He had always thought she was very attractive. Now seeing her here, outside the bank and dressed more casually than at the bank, she was even more attractive. Wow! Stunning is the word that came to mind. He couldn't think of a strong enough adjective to describe her. Whatever was beyond beautiful, that was Tracy.

Walking to the car, he asked how her day was.

"Not too bad," she said. A normal Friday. We are always a little busier than other days of the week. People cashing paychecks, getting ready for the weekend."

"Makes sense," he said as he quickened his pace to get slightly in front of her to open the passenger door. A minute later they were on their way to Umami Moto. About two minutes from the restaurant, she asked, "Where are we going anyway?" They were only two minutes from the restaurant and it struck him that he had never even asked if she like sushi.

"I was thinking Umami Moto, but I'm sorry, I completely forgot to ask if you even like sushi." He realized by the way she started to frown up her face, that was probably a no and he had made his first faux pas of the evening.

"I don't really care for sushi," she said. As he started stammering, trying to explain that they could go elsewhere, she laughed a little and said, "I'm joking. I love sushi and I have heard that Umami Moto is great."

"Ah, very funny, Ms. Tracy, you got me. You got me good. Just for that I'm turning around and headed to Wendy's. We'll just split a junior bacon cheeseburger and call it a night."

"Shoot, that works for me, I like a good hamburger, too."

They both had a good laugh.

Sitting down for dinner, they fell into an easy conversation. They talked about high school, living in Milwaukee, hobbies and their families. He loved the fact that she was easy to talk to. Very easy to talk to. For dinner, they both had the Miso Soup to start, and for the entrée, she had the Snapper Salad while he tried the Shitake Roll. Everything they had both heard about the restaurant was accurate. The food and the service were both outstanding. Halfway to his mouth with the last bite of his Shitake Roll, she asked, "So why do you deal weed?"

Kind of like the other night at Caine's, his mind started racing.

"Talk about being at a complete loss for words," Marcus finally blurted out.

"Maybe that was the objective," Tracy confided. While he had given some thought to potentially having this conversation with her one day, she had caught him completely off guard. He hadn't planned on having it this soon. How did she know? What were her feelings about it? Was this the first and last date? And now that he had been just sitting there for what felt like five minutes, what should he say? After re-engaging his brain, he figured the best approach was to be completely honest.

"My side hustle, dealing weed, is the means that serves – if not justifies – my end goals: establishing an emergency fund, paying for college and building a financial foundation for my retirement. The reality is that the only other way I can go to college is to take out a significant amount of money in loans; and I have no desire to be saddled with debt from student loans long after I've graduated. As far as the emergency fund, it's the money I keep in a savings account … "

"I was wondering why you had both a savings and checking account."

"Yeah, that account is just to meet unexpected expenses. Should something out of the ordinary come up, I won't need to dip into the money I'm saving for college and retirement. It is really just insurance to make sure I can stay on track to meet my financial goals."

"Retirement? I don't believe I have ever met somebody around our own age that was talking about retirement already."

"I'm not trying to retire by 35 or anything like that. And because my primary focus is on saving for college, I don't have a lot of money in my retirement account right now. However, I do think it is important to get started and lay the foundation as early as possible."

Looking a little sheepish, Tracy said, "I'm a little embarrassed to admit that even though I work in a bank I don't know anything about investing in the stock market and I only know a little bit more about retirement accounts. I know there are 401(k)s and IRAs. The Traditional and the other one, the uh, the uh … "

"The Roth IRA," said Marcus, finishing the thought for her.

"Yeah, that's it," she confirmed.

"Are you participating in the 401(k) plan at the bank? I assume they offer one."

"Yes they do. They absolutely do. But I have to admit that I'm not. While money would be tight, I could probably find a little extra money to commit to a retirement plan. However, the truth is I got all the documentation from our HR department but I haven't gotten around to really looking into it, taking the time to understand all the details."

"No doubt it can be tight, but it really is in your best interest to look into it and get started soon as possible."

"I figure I've got time. It can't be that big a difference if I wait awhile to get it started."

"Not necessarily," said Marcus, shaking his head. "I'll give you a quick example of how important it is to start early. Imagine twin sisters. We'll call them Macy and Tracy. Way back in the day when the twins were 28 years old, they had a conversation regarding savings and investments. Macy let her sister know that she had managed to reduce her debt and was prepared to invest $1,000 a year. Unfortunately, Tracy had not reduced her debt and was not in a position to invest any of her income. Jump ahead seven years when the twins are 35 years old. Macy had been investing $1,000 during that time, earned 10% annually on her investments and is now sitting on a portfolio that is almost $10,500. During the previous seven years, poor Tracy was not able to invest anything."

"Yeah, Poor Tracy is right."

"It gets better though."

"Well good," said Tracy.

Continuing, Marcus said, "Fortunately however, she is now at the point where she is able and prepared to invest $1,000 every year. While Tracy is just now starting to invest, Macy decides that she is no longer interested in contributing new money to her investment accounts. Now, that is not something I would recommend, but it makes the story a little more dramatic. Fortunately however, she does decide to leave the $10,500 in place."

"So let's summarize," said Marcus.

"Shoot, I can do that," offered Tracy. "Macy invested $1,000 a year for seven years at a 10% rate of return, which resulted in almost $10,500. While she decided to stop investing, she left the money in place, letting it ride, and earned 10% each year for the next 25 years. So she invested $7,000. How much did she have at the end?"

"Hold on, slow your roll, we'll get there."

"What about Tracy? Poor Tracy?" asked Marcus.

"Poor Tracy did not invest any money during the seven years that Macy did," said Tracy. "However, she did start contributing to her retirement accounts at the same time her sister stopped, faithfully contributing $1,000 annually for the next 25 years. So in the end, she invested a total of $25,000. If my math is right, and I'm pretty sure it is, she contributed $18,000 more than her sister. My guess is that even though Macy contributed $18,000 less, because she started earlier, she would end up with more money."

"How right you are, Tracy. I forget the exact numbers, and I don't have a compound interest calculator in my head, but basically, even though Macy contributed $18,000 less, she ends up with about $5,000 more than Tracy when they 60."

"Wow! That is seriously crazy"

"Yep, it really is. That is the power of time and compound interest."

"Going back to IRAs for a minute, I'm sure someone told me at one point, but what's the difference between the Traditional and Roth IRA again?"

"They're similar in that you can contribute the same amount to both - $5,500 - when you're 49 and younger; and catch up contributions - an additional $1,000 - starting in the year you turn 50. The differences have to do with taxes. With a Traditional IRA, you get a tax break during the years you are making contributions. You don't pay taxes until you start withdrawing the money, after age 59½. It's what they call a tax-deferred type of account."

"With a Roth IRA, you pay taxes during the years you're making contributions. However, when you start withdrawing the money – at 59½, the same age as the Traditional IRA – you don't have to pay any taxes since you've already paid. It's what they call tax-exempt. Everything that I have read suggests that if you don't have access to a 401(k), which I don't at McDonald's, an IRA is the best way for a young person to save for retirement. I started mine, a Roth, about a year ago."

"Really?" Tracy seemed impressed.

"Well, like I said, I don't plan to retire any time soon, but I did want to get my foundation in place."

"How did you learn so much?"

"By reading stuff on my own, mostly. Anytime I came across a finance related magazine, like at a doctor's office, I read it; I bought a couple books about investing and retirement that I had heard about; and I follow three or four personal finance blogs online. There is a lot of good information out there that is basically free. I don't know where the initial interest really came from, but the more I learn, the more I'm convinced it's important to get a handle on your money. The sooner, the better."

"So how long you plan on doing the hustle thing? The side hustle as you call it?"

"Well, I just met my emergency fund goal. Like I said, that's the money in the savings account, and I need about $14,000 more to meet my college savings goal."

"$14,000!?" Tracy exclaimed. "Wow. That's not chump change."

"No it isn't. My plan is to save it within the next year and then quit the hustle. Like I said, I don't necessarily like doing it, but I have some definitive goals and if doing this for a little longer helps me to get there, I'll do it. What do you think about it?"

"Well to tell you the truth, I wasn't sure you did when I asked. I had mentioned you to a girl I know a little bit - she works at that bakery by the bank - and she said she thought you might deal. I didn't know what to think. You didn't come across to me as some crazy thug and you were always nice when you came into the bank. I wasn't gonna say anything. It just kind of slipped out. I figured it couldn't hurt to go out with you at least once."

"Just once?" Marcus asked.

"Well, I think a second date might be doable, Mr. Williams. Continue being a gentleman and I like your chances." Of course she wouldn't say it to him, but there was no doubt that the energy between them was palpable.

After they decided against dessert, Marcus asked for the check.

"Got your half?" Marcus asked with a straight face.

"Uh, yeah, let me just ..." Tracy started to say.

"Ha, I'm messing with you, girl."

"I see. Very funny. Very, very funny." A few minutes later they were in the car and headed to her house.

About halfway there, Tracy turned to him, "Do you bowl?"

"Do I bowl?" Yeah, occasionally. I ain't in a league or anything, but I have been known to break 200 on occasion."

"Really?"

"No, not really. I think my all-time high game is like 164 or 165. Something like that."

"Take a right here," she blurted out at the last minute. Barely in time, Marcus made the turn. "There's a bowling alley two blocks up," she said. "You game?"

"Yeah, I'm game. I'm ready, willing and able."

Two hours later they were back on their way to her house. Marcus had crushed her in all three games that they played. He vowed to never let her forget it. "Don't feel too bad. I'm sure you just had an off day. You almost broke 75 in the second game."

"Oh, you're funny," she said. Pulling in front of her house, Marcus jumped out, ran around the rear of the car to the passenger side and opened her door. "Why thank you, Mr. Williams."

"You're very welcome, Ms. Jackson." Walking her to her door, that nervousness washed over him again. Even in this cold ass air he felt his pores open up as if he was on the verge of sweating. *Deep breath, Marcus, be cool*, he thought to himself.

"I had a good time. I'm glad you decided to give me a chance."

"So am I. It was fun. Thank you."

After an awkward minute, he started to lean forward. She stood firm. Finishing his movement, Marcus gave her a kiss on the cheek.

"Goodnight, Tracy."

"Goodnight, Marcus." Halfway back to the car, he glanced back. She was still on the porch. She had not moved.

"Call you tomorrow?"

"You better."

[9] THE DECISION

Waking up just before the alarm sounded, Marcus reached over and shut off the clock before it did. He really need to get a new alarm clock. This one was just way too loud. Laying there for a minute or so, he mentally ran through the date with Tracy last night. It probably went about as well as it could have. Umami Moto was great and her idea to go bowling after dinner was perfect.

As much as anything, he was relieved that she wasn't put off by his side hustle. A lot of people have preconceived ideas about drugs and those that deal them. His experience had been that people often judged the decisions of others without knowing what options they had at the time. He was glad to know that she had an open mind and could appreciate what he was trying to do.

Before anything else this morning, he had to get Train's car back to him. He needed it for work later. After throwing on some jeans, a hoodie and his shoes, he grabbed his phone and sent off a quick text: *to Train – leaving here in 10 minutes*. The reply was almost immediate. It was almost as if Train was sittin' there staring at the phone's screen, ready to pounce as soon as a message came in. His phone beeped with notification of the text reply: *from Train – sounds good I'm ready*.

Making his way to the kitchen, he grabbed a glass of water and turned on the coffee maker. He wasn't that hungry, so he'd probably go without a smoothie or a bowl of cereal this morning. Just a cup of coffee would do. Take it in a little travel mug with him. Standing there waiting for the coffee to brew, he reviewed his plans for the day in his head. No Mickey D's today. Although he was willing to work more hours, and had asked for a few more this week, Vanessa wasn't willing – or able? – to give him some more. That left only a few deliveries today. Going back to his phone and reviewing his text messages, he confirmed that he only had five; and he didn't need to head out to the first one for another three hours or so.

As soon as the coffee was finished brewing, he added some cream and sugar; and poured the caramel colored nectar into his favorite, well his only, travel mug. Grabbing his wallet and keys, he was out the door. Train stepped out as soon as he pulled up. He must have been keeping an eye out the window. He parked and slid over so that Train could drive. Jumping in and turning the car around, Train pointed the car back toward the Square.

"So how was the date, my man?"

"It was good. Real good. After we ate at Umami Moto, I was taking her home, thinking that was the night. Instead, she suggested we go bowling."

"Bowling?" Train asked.

"Yeah, bowing. Believe me, I was surprised. It has been awhile since I last bowled. We had a good time. We even talked about my side hustle."

"Oh, really? She's cool with it?"

"I mean, she wasn't thrilled about it, but I explained my rationale and kind of explained my plan. She thought it made sense. Based on the way the night ended and the fact that she wants me to call, I believe we're good. I guess we'll see."

"Sounds good, Marcus. Real good."

Back at the Square, he thanked Train for the use of his car and ran up to his apartment. It was a little cold this morning. Although he should probably run this morning, he decided against it. Instead, he would just get a little ab work and a good stretch from head to toe. A quick change in the bedroom and then he moseyed into the living room, docking his iPhone to his stereo.

Scrolling to his 'workout' playlist, he turned the volume up and fell to the floor to start his ab work. Had to maintain a strong core. He figured he would start with the Bicycle, three sets of 15 repetitions. Next up were some Vertical Leg Crunches, as with the Bicycle, three sets of 15 repetitions. Taking a little break, he quickly headed to the kitchen to grab a drink of water.

Back in the living room, next up were some Long Arm Crunches, three sets of 10 repetitions. Following the Long Arm Crunches were some Reverse Crunches, three sets of 10 repetitions. Concluding the workout, Marcus did three sets, 10 repetitions each of Side Jackknifes. With his stomach a little tight, he started his stretch routine with holding the Cobra Pose for one minute, taking a break, and then holding it for another 30 seconds. Ten minutes later, stretched out and feeling more relaxed, he grabbed a tall glass of orange juice and made his way back to the living room.

With time to kill, he turned off the stereo and turned on the TV, deciding against CNBC or Bloomberg TV this morning. Instead he figured he would catch a good action or thriller movie on Netflix. Scrolling through the available movies, he settled on *Training Day*, an oldie but a goodie. You couldn't really go wrong with Denzel. Just over two hours later, the movie ended, he turned off the TV and headed to his bedroom to get ready.

Thirty minutes later, he was out the door with his backpack slung over his shoulder. No sooner had he walked out the door and turned the corner that he ran into Carl.

"What up, kid?"

"You know, just doing what I do."

"I was hoping I ran into you. Can I get a bag?"

"Yeah, of course you can get a bag."

"Cool, but I don't have my money with me."

"Don't have it with you or don't have any? C'mon, Carl. You know I don't extend credit. You gotta pay as you go. You got something for me or not?"

"No, man. I'll have to try to hook up with you tomorrow."

"Sounds good. And I'll hook you up then. I gotta get going."

Based on the locations of his deliveries, Marcus thought he would take the bus to the most distant location, the bus to the second location and walk home from there, hitting the last three while working his way home. The weather wasn't too bad today. The fresh air and the walking – particularly since he didn't run this morning – would be good for him. Making his way to the stop, he had a 10 minute wait before the bus finally showed up. Jumping on, he was immediately knocked back by the smell. "Damn! Somebody had the funk hanging off of 'em bad. Getting as far away from the smell as he could, he headed straight to the back. Even Rosa Parks would have gladly sat in the back today.

The bus dropped him two blocks from his first delivery, Rickee, a painter. Approaching Rickee's door, it appeared to magically open as he got closer. But just like that, Rickee filled the empty space holding a bag of trash. Turns out it wasn't magic at all, just trash day.

"What up, Marcus?"

"Not too much, Rickee."

"Come on in, man. I'll be right back. I just need to take this down to the dumpster." While he waited, he checked out some of Rickee's new pieces. He didn't know much about painting, but the stuff he had seen in Rickee's apartment looked pretty good to him.

"Sorry, had to get that trash out. It was starting to stink."

"No worse than that damn bus this morning."

"The bus?"

"Nothing man, just thinking out loud. How ya been?"

"Not bad. Like everybody else, just working hard. Trying to keep my head above water."

"How are things going with the paintings? You had mentioned before that you were putting some on consignment."

"Going well. In fact, a little better than I thought. I won't be reaching millionaire status and kicking it with Jay-Z and Beyonce any time soon, but I won't be missing any meals either."

"Cool," Said Marcus. "I hope things continue to work out for you." Reaching into his backpack, he pulled out two baggies and handed them to Rickee. With his money in hand, he made his way to the front door.

"Take care, man. We'll talk soon."

"Bet," said Rickee.

Back to the bust stop, he waited with a group of three other people for a bus that was apparently running late. Four minutes past its scheduled time, it finally showed up. Sitting on the bus, he pulled out his phone and sent a quick text message: *to Tracy – great time last night movie tomorrow?* He knew she was working, so he didn't expect a reply for awhile.

Jumping off at his stop, he made the five minute walk to John's. Ringing the bell, he waited the minute until the door was answered.

"Hey," John said, sounding surprised. "What's up Marcus?" At that very second, Marcus realized he had the wrong John. This was John P. He meant to deliver to John D.

"Shit, I'm sorry, John."

"Yeah, I wasn't expecting you today."

"I know. I got my wires a little crossed. I apologize."

"Not a problem. Since you're here, I could use a bag if you have it."

"Yeah, I do." Stepping inside, they conducted the unplanned transaction quickly and then Marcus was on his way. The bad news was that he was now running behind his scheduled time at John D's. He prided himself on his punctuality. The good news was that he was within two blocks of where he should have gone in the first place. Three minutes later he was knocking on John D's door.

"Hey, come on in, Marcus. Right on time." Peeking at his watch, Marcus saw that he was really about six or seven minutes late. *Going to the wrong house. That had never happened to me*, he thought. Oh well, he wasn't that late and John D. was cool. Wrapping up their transaction quickly, no small talk today, Marcus was in and out within two minutes.

The first two, and one unplanned, deliveries out of the way, Marcus was walking the last three, making his way back toward the Square. The next two, P.J. and Tina, stayed in the same complex. That made delivery very easy. Both were home and paid quickly. He had a brief convo with P.J. about gaming – P.J. was playing a new Xbox One game when he walked in

– but the transaction with Tina was largely void of words. Apparently she was in a hurry. That wasn't a problem for Marcus.

Leaving their complex, Marcus made the turn for home. Just then a text message: *from Tracy – movie sounds good your choice call later*. He texted her back: *to Tracy – will do*. He was feeling pretty good before, now he felt great. It was a beautiful day! It felt like it was even warming up a bit. The sound of a gunshot in the distance – it sounded like it came from behind him – startled him out of his brief day dream. Putting a little pep in his step, he quickened his pace to the last delivery, Alix. Minutes later, there were sirens heading the opposite way. Yep, it appeared as if the gunshot came from somewhere opposite of the direction he was traveling.

Reaching the lobby, with its secure doorway that led into the foyer, Marcus rang Alix' apartment. Twenty seconds later, she buzzed him up. A producer at 99.1 – The Mix, he was introduced to Alix by Eric. She was fine. In fact, she was real fine. But the cool thing was she didn't act like it. She always carried herself in a down to Earth way. He would guess that she was in her late twenties, maybe early thirties, and based on some of their conversations, had what sounded like a good job that she enjoyed. She had a chance to meet a lot of the artists that came to town and he assumed she made pretty good coin.

As he reached the landing on the third floor, her door opened before he had a chance to knock.

"Come on in. What's going on, Marcus?"

"Not too much, Alix. Just out enjoying my Saturday afternoon. What's going on with you?"

"Work, work and more work. That's about it."

"Well you need to get out a little bit more. They say there is more to life than just work."

"So true," she said. "That is what they say."

"No male friend to take you out for a nice evening?"

"Not at this time, male or female, unfortunately."

What? He thought. *Did she play that way?* It was cool with him if she did, he didn't have that hang up like a lot of people did.

"And you? Any female friends?"

"Kinda."

"What do you mean, kinda?"

"Just started something. Took her out for the first time last night."

"Well good for you. Where did you go?"

"Dinner at Umami Moto."

"How was it? I don't care for sushi but I hear it's excellent."

"It is. Very good. Supposed to see her tomorrow. A movie. Any suggestions? See anything good lately?"

"I wish I could help, my friend. It's probably been two months since I've seen anything."

Reaching into his backpack, Marcus handed over two baggies as she walked over to the kitchen table and grabbed her purse. After briefly rummaging through it she handed him the money.

"Well alright, Alix. Like Dorothy I gotta ease on down the road."

"Alright. Thanks, Marcus and watch out for them crazy-ass flying monkeys," she said as she opened the door. Down the stairs, out the foyer and he was on his way home. A good afternoon.

Marcus stopped at Taco Bell on the way home. It was close, he was hungry and he didn't have much to eat at the house. He might as well satisfy his hunger with a little Americanized Mexican food. "Where else could you get chalupas and gorditas, that large, on the cheap?" While he wasn't certain, his guess was chalupas and gorditas were real foods. However, he was pretty sure they didn't taste anything like the chalupas and gorditas served in Mexico City, Nogales or Agua Prieta.

But hey, he thought to himself, *they're cheap*. And as far as he was concerned, cheap was good. Hell, he was on a budget. Making his way through the front door, he stepped right to the counter – he must have caught a lull – and ordered two chicken gorditas, a beef taco and a drink. No chalupa today. Carrying his tray of food and drink to the rear most table, he plopped down onto a hard plastic chair and dug right in. He must have been even more hungry than he thought. After the gorditas and taco were gone, he headed right back to the counter and picked up another taco. Expanding his palette, he ordered the chicken taco for the second round.

Stuffed, kind of like a chalupa, Marcus made his way home. Not much going on tonight. He was done with deliveries for the day. He had minimized his time at his spots since his encounter with Caine, so he didn't plan on hitting the street tonight. He would call Train, but he was working. It looked like it was going to be a solo, quiet night at the apartment. Plus, he might as well take it easy tonight. Tomorrow would be a busy one. He planned to run in the morning, he had a midday shift, 10 a.m. – 2 p.m., at McDonald's and of course, a movie tomorrow night with Tracy.

The next day got off to a great start. He had an excellent run - waiting till it got a little warmer, a little later - before heading out. He wasn't in a hurry since he didn't work till later. Work was good. It was busy, a typical lunch time crowd, but there was no drama.

Getting back home, he headed to his bedroom to change. A little more comfortable, he headed to the living room, kicked back on the couch and turned on the TV. They had agreed to just meet at the theater; the Humphrey IMAX Dome Theater over on West Wells Street. Figuring he should confirm the time, he sent her a text: *to Tracy – movie starts at 7:20 meet at 6:50?* Fifteen minutes later he got his reply text: *from Tracy – sounds perfect see ya there.*

Leaving the apartment a little bit earlier than necessary, he wanted to get to the theater in time to get the tickets so they wouldn't have to wait outside. Things worked out perfectly. He bought their tickets and then waited in the lobby, keeping an eye out the window. About six minutes later he spotted her, looking around for him. Stepping out the door, he waved when she looked his way. Meeting him inside, she immediately gave him a hug.

"Perfect timing," he said. "I've already bought the tickets. You wanna get something to snack on? Something to drink?"
"Sounds good. What are we seeing anyway?"
"*The Equalizer* starring Denzel and directed by Antoine Fuqua."
"Didn't he direct *Training Day*?"
"Yep. And *Brooklyn's Finest, Olympus Has Fallen* and some other stuff."
Stopping at the concession stand, they picked up some popcorn, licorice and water. The movie was great and they had a good time. Marcus walked her to her bus stop where they talked about her job and more about her family while they waited for the bus. With the bus approaching, Marcus gave her a kiss and a nice long hug. *Damn those lips are soft*, he thought. As she climbed aboard, he let her know that he would call soon.
"Have a good night, Tracy."
"You too," she said. "Be safe going home."

As he turned and started to make his way to his bus stop, he saw Drake's sedan parked in a lot across the street. *Had it been there the entire time?* he thought, questioning himself. *How could I have missed it?* Just as he spotted the car, Drake flashed the parking lots. Marcus thought about ignoring him and simply going on about his business.

However, he knew he would have to deal with Drake and Cain before long, so there was no point in ignoring him now. Plus, he had basically already made up his mind, knew what he planned to do, and besides, he still had another couple days before his decision was due. He had started to cross the street but there was no need. The headlights in the sedan came on and Drake pulled the car out of the lot, hung a U-turn just down the street and pulled up in front of him, stopping suddenly as the passenger side window came down.

"Get in." Making a quick U-turn, Drake sped away from the bus stop in the opposite direction.

There was no need for Drake to conspicuously reveal the butt of his weapon or otherwise try to threaten or intimidate Marcus. He was ready to deal with this.

"What up, Marcus?"

"Nothing. What do you need?"

"Caine wants an answer."

"Now? He said a week. I still have a couple more days."

"He changed his mind. You've had enough time. Things are moving quickly. So what's it going to be?"

After a brief silence.

"I'm gonna have to pass. I don't see a lot of upside in working for somebody else."

"You sure that's the route you want to go, Marcus? Are you really sure? If so, remember, you're now done with your hustle. Effectively immediately. No exceptions and no second chances."

"I'm sure."

With that, Drake pulled over abruptly. So abruptly in fact, the car behind him swerved quickly to the left to avoid him and indicated their displeasure with two quick blasts from their horn.

"Out! And remember, effectively immediately, no exceptions and no second chances."

"Asshole!" Marcus cursed under his breath as Drake pulled out into traffic. He had dropped him off even further from his apartment which meant he had to hustle back to the bus stop so he could catch the bus home. And it was getting colder. "Asshole!" he cursed at the night.

[10] FRAMED

Startled awake by the blare of his alarm clock, Marcus rolled over and smacked the snooze button. Seven minutes later, he hit the snooze again. When the alarm went off for the third time, he went ahead and hit the off button. He sat up and let his feet fall to the floor. He had slept like shit and had a headache. He supposed the encounter with Drake was what was weighing on his mind. Although he knew he made the only choice he could, he also knew that the hard part was just starting.

He had decided that he was not going to work for Caine. That had been decided immediately. The only real internal question was would he give up the hustle altogether? In the end, he decided not to give up the hustle completely, but to modify it. While he hated to do it, he was going to give up the street piece. The elimination of one of his streams of income would impact his bottom line of course, certainly in the short-term. However, he planned to actively work to increase the customer base of the delivery service.

While he may not be able to make up for all the revenue that was lost, he could certainly mitigate the losses. While not ideal, it should keep him off of Caine's radar. What he wasn't able to calculate, at this point, was how much longer he would have to maintain the hustle – the now reduced hustle – before he would meet his goals and be in a position to make his exit from the Cream City.

Train swung by later that morning and Marcus filled him in on last night happenings. First the good.

"I met Tracy over at the IMAX Theater and we … "

"The Humphrey Dome over on West Wells Street?"

"Yeah."

"Nice theater. Sorry about the interruption. Go ahead, man."

"So we met at the theater and saw that new Denzel movie, *The Equalizer.*"

"Was it any good?"

"Absolutely. A good action thriller. You should go check it out. Take your girl Renee out one night."

"I don't know, man. You know I'm on a budget."

"You're always talking 'bout being on a budget. Hell, even people on a budget have to allot a little bit of money for entertainment and fun."

"True. So true."

"So the date with Tracy was cool. Just like I knew it would be. That was the good."

"And the bad?" asked Train.

"That fool Drake, I told you about."

"Oh shit. What happened?"

"After Tracy's bus pulled away, I was getting ready to head to my stop and I saw Drake's sedan parked in a lot across the street. No sooner had I spotted him than he flashed his parking lights to get my attention. The next thing I know, he hangs a U-turn just down the street and pulled up in front of me, driving like some kind of crazy man."

"What did he say?"

"He told me to get in the car, which I did, and then basically he ran down how I had to make the decision right then and there."

"I thought that Caine was giving you a week or something?"

"That's what I thought and that's what I said to Drake. Apparently, Caine had changed his mind and wanted an answer right then and there, which was cool, because like I told you from the beginning, working for him was never really an option for me."

"So I told him I was gonna have to pass. Told him I didn't see a whole lot of upside in working for somebody else. He pressed me a little bit. Asked if I was sure that's what I wanted to do. That was it really. At the end he just warned me that I had to quit my hustle immediately."

"So I assume you aren't going to just quit. What's your plan?"

"Hold on," said Marcus, as he reached for his phone: *from Ma – if you aren't working you should come by for dinner tonight about 6.* Pounding a quick reply: *to Ma – sounds good see ya 2night.*

" I'm going to modify the hustle, not give it up. I'm going to let go of the street piece and focus just on the delivery service. Giving up the street piece will lower my revenue, but I'm hoping to add some delivery clients. I probably can't make up all the money that is going to be lost, but I figure I can mitigate the damage. It ain't ideal, but it should keep me off Caine's radar."

"Sounds like a smart play," said Train. "Stay off the streets. Let him have it."

"Well, I have to get up out of here," Train said, "I'm supposed to take Renee out for lunch and then I have a short shift at work tonight."

"Cool," said Marcus. "Looks like a slow day for me. I don't have a shift at Mickey D's until tomorrow afternoon."

"Alright, kid. Be cool and I'll talk at ya later," said Train as he made his way to the door. "If you're working tomorrow, maybe we'll grab some lunch the following day."

"Sounds good. I'll talk to ya later, man."

Heading to the kitchen to get a glass of juice, his phone rang.

"Maybe it's Tracy," he thought. Hoped. No luck. It was Vanessa from work.

"Hello, Marcus."

"Vanessa. How you doing?"

"I'm well, thanks for asking. Can you come in this afternoon? I had two people call in sick."

"What time?" he asked. Then he thought to himself, *what am I thinking? It's not like I have something else going on this afternoon. Does the time really matter?*

"I could really use you from 12:00 to 5:00."

"Sure, Vanessa. I can make it this afternoon."

"I appreciate it, Marcus. See you later. Bye."

Well, so much for nothing this afternoon, he thought. Considering he had about two hours before he had to leave, he plopped down on the couch and turned on the TV. He still had a slight headache and just wanted to relax before heading to work. Take it easy. He figured he would just go straight from work to his parents for dinner. Just needed to pack a change of clothes in his back pack and he would be good to go.

About an hour and a half later, he peeled himself off the couch and started to get ready. Soon after, with his clothes changed, deodorant on, teeth brushed and a change of clothes in the backpack, he was ready to go. Realizing he nearly forgot his wallet, he ran back to the bedroom and picked it up. Now he was ready and out the door he went.

Similar to a few days ago, it was a long, long day at work. If everything didn't go wrong, it was certainly most things. Vanessa put him on the front counter with Vijay. Although he was fairly new, he wasn't brand new! He should have been able to handle the high volume of customers. He didn't think it was possible, but it appeared as if Vijay was slower than Barb. Not only was he slow, it seemed like he messed up every third or fourth order, requiring a void and a redo on the transaction. All time consuming.

"You alright, Vijay?" Marcus asked when they had a momentary lull.

"Sorry, Marcus. I have a lot going on at home and I can't concentrate as well as I should. My apologies."

"Don't worry about it, man. Just slow it down a little bit and take a deep breath or two if you start to feel a little anxious. We've all been there." While not perfect, Vijay seemed to settle down a little and find a good rhythm.

Whereas two homeless dudes threw down in the lobby the other day, this time it was two crewmembers. It didn't quite come to blows, but apparently there was a serious disagreement between Shaundra and Cherelle, who were both working the Meats station. He never did hear what the fuss was about, but fortunately Vanessa got there in time, before chicken nuggets and hamburger patties stated flying. Vanessa had Shaundra switch with Paul, who was working the Lobby Station, and had Cherelle switch with Zane, who was working drive-thru. Crisis averted, everyone got back to work and things were fine for awhile.

But as the old saying goes, that was only the calm before the storm. As soon as it looked like he might be able to finish his shift without any more drama, he caught the slightest scent of shit. It had to be coming from one of the bathrooms. He was wrong. It was both. No sooner had the smell started to waft toward the lobby, Shay came back into the kitchen area and let Vanessa know that they had toilet issues in both the men's and women's bathrooms.

Apparently some kids had coordinated some type of attack on the toilets, clogging them up simultaneously. Of course, it doesn't help when people keep using the toilets as if they were working. By the time the problem was realized, there was quite a mess in both bathrooms.

The problem was so bad, Vanessa tackled the women's bathroom herself and asked Marcus, whom she trusted more than anyone else, to handle the men's room. Once Shaundra came up to take his place at the front counter, he took a deep breath, likely the last deep breathe he could draw for awhile, and headed into battle.

While it wasn't as bad as he thought it might be, nor take as long as he thought it might, he was awfully glad when he was finished. When he was done, he literally sprinted out of the bathroom. During the entire crisis, maybe 15 minutes, most customers seemed to be oblivious. Other than a few who wrinkled up their noses and looked around curiously, most seemed to stay completely engaged with either their cell phones, their Big Macs and fries or all three.

Finishing his last 30 minutes back at the front counter, he was glad to be going when it was time to punch out. *Another day in the salt mine*, he thought. Definitely a tough one. Changing clothes right after punching out, he bid everyone a good night. Both Vanessa and Vijay made a point to thank him as he made his way to the door.

"No problem. You guys take care and we'll see ya soon." Now, on to what should turn out to be the best part of his day. Spending time with the family.

Arriving at his folk's house, he quickly greeted everyone. A hug and a kiss for Ma, hugs for Pops and Marlon.

"How is everybody?"

"We're good, Baby," said his mother, as she made her way back to the kitchen. "Come on in and get comfortable. We're going to eat in about 20 minutes."

"Sounds good. What are we having?"

"A salad with fresh spinach – your father needs more green, leafy vegetables – some macaroni and cheese, and grilled chicken breasts. For dessert, I'm trying out a new recipe for low-fat custard. Your father could use less ... "

"Alright, Marie, I think the boys get the point," said his father, lounging comfortably in his favorite chair. Marcus and Marlon just laughed.

As always, dinner was outstanding, particularly since his father didn't press him on his plans for getting a better job, saving money for college and everything else. They followed dinner with a family game of Mexican Train Dominoes. They had quite the game, getting down to 0's, it was close. They were all within 50 points of each other. It was likely that whoever won this last set, would win the game.

Marcus' mother, who rarely won, and often simply resorted to accusing everyone of cheating or claiming the three boys were beating up on her, staged a dramatic comeback. Just when it looked like Marlon was going to win, he was forced into a position to draw numerous dominoes, racking up unwanted points, and their mother ended up beating Marlon by five points. You would have thought she won a world title or something. She even got up and did a little dominoes dance.

"Please stop dancing, mother, you're going to hurt somebody," Marcus chided her.

"Or throw a hip out," Marcus suggested.

Their father just sat back and laughed.

After a great dinner and dominoes, Marcus was ready to call it a night. Just as he was preparing to head out, make his way to the bus stop, his father offered him a ride.

"Hold on, Marcus, let me grab my coat and keys, I'll give you a ride." He was speechless. In all the time since he had moved out, he could only remember one other time his father had given him a ride back to his apartment. On that occasion, the middle of last winter, it was cold as hell and his mother insisted her husband take their son home.

"Thanks, Pops. Sounds good." After the obligatory kisses and hugs to his mother and Marlon, they were on their way.

Marcus had half expected the barrage of questions to come once they were alone. He was wrong. His father kept the conversation very light.

"How's work, son?"

"Not too bad. Some days are drama-free and others are just the opposite. Today was one of those days. The guy I was working the front counter with was slow, which meant I had to assist two to three guests for his every one. Two of the female crew members almost got in a fight while preparing meats … "

"What!?"

"Yep. Fortunately, the manager, Vanessa, got 'em separated before we had an episode in the restaurant. And a little bit before I was scheduled to leave, some would be comedians clogged up the toilets, making a mess in both the women's and men's bathrooms. Believe me, I was glad to get out of there today."

Pulling in front of the Square, his father suggested he be careful.

"I'm glad to see that this area is coming around a little bit, but it is still kind of rough around the edges, so watch your back. Be careful."

"Will do, Pop. Take care and have a good night."

"You too, son." Wow, he didn't know what quite to make of the offer of a ride and that conversation, but he wasn't going to think too much about it and search for some kind of deep meaning. All he knew that it was good to simply have a conversation with his father, absent of any tension. *Overall a very good day*, he thought to himself as he bounded up the stairs to his apartment.

"So what do you think, Cuz?" Drake asked Caine.

"Keep an eye on him. Do it from a distance though. He's smart, so he'll probably do the smart thing and get out of the game completely. However, he might just be too smart for his own damn good. If he deals, in any way, shape or form, carry out what we talked about. I want the message sent loud and clear. I don't want there to be any doubt that when Caine speaks, Caine means what he says."

The next couple of days went by like a blur. Train and Tracy were working quite a bit, so while he had exchanged a number of text messages with both, he hadn't seen either of them. Hopefully that would change soon. He had talked with Tracy about trying to carve out some time tomorrow night; however, her folks had some distant relatives coming into town, so she couldn't commit to anything.

As he had planned, and shared with Train, he hadn't dealt on the street since his last encounter with Drake. Things were going well with the delivery service. So far, so good since the mandated change in business practices. Over the last two days, in addition to watching a lot of Netflix, he had made deliveries to 13 or 14 clients. Janice had even brought in some new business for him, a co-worker named Alvin.

It turned out that Alvin shared a building with Alix, of 99.1 – The Mix fame. On his way there now, Marcus looked forward to meeting him and getting their first transaction done. When you were dealing drugs, there was always some apprehension when dealing with someone new, even if the introduction was made by a reliable, at least what was believed to be, a reliable source.

Reaching the lobby, with its secure doorway which led into the foyer, Marcus rang Alvin's apartment. Almost immediately, he buzzed him up. That was a good sign. Reaching the landing on the second floor, Alvin opened the door after one quick knock.

"Come on in. Marcus?"

"Indeed. Good to meet you, Alvin."

"Good to meet you too, Marcus. Janice speaks highly of you. Says you're very professional, which is good to know."

"Thank you. Am I correct in that you want to start with a couple of bags?"

"Yes. That should work."

"Did Janice explain the pricing structure or would you like me to go over it?"

"Yes and no. Yes, she did explain. No, I don't think it's necessary to go over it again. It sounds reasonable to me."

"Cool," said Marcus, reaching into his back pack, grabbing two baggies." Alvin produced the money and just like that, their first transaction was in the books.

"You'll likely hear from me in a week or so," said Alvin as he opened the door for Marcus.

"That works. Talk to you soon." With that he headed down the stairs and out the foyer he went.

Checking the text he received while he was concluding business with Alvin, Marcus saw that Estelle was hoping for a delivery tonight. While he normally required six hours notification prior to a delivery, he could make an exception for Estelle. He had the extra product in his back pack, he was already out and her place wasn't that far. And most importantly, she was his favorite customer. He was a little surprised she was ready for more product. Normally two baggies would last her another three or four days. It's likely her back was really acting up and she had gone through her supply a little faster to help manage the pain.

Pulling his Packers cap a little lower and yanking the coat's zipper to the top, he bundled up tightly and headed over to North 26th Street as the temperature started to drop a little. Reaching Estelle's place about 15 minutes later, he pulled open the screen and tapped lightly. Nothing after about a minute. Tapping a little harder, he waited another minute. Turning his hand 90 degrees, he struck the door a little harder with the side of his fist. It swung partially open.

Opening the door wider and stepping in, Marcus called out.
"Estelle? it's Marcus." Nothing.
"Hello?" The light from the stove was on, but it appeared as if Estelle wasn't here. *Oh shit*, he thought, *maybe she had an accident; fell, a stroke or something?* Reaching for the lamp on the closest end table, he turned it on, lighting up the room. "Estelle?" he called out. Nothing. Walking past the kitchen, toward the bedroom, he saw a foot out of the corner of his eye. *Shit, she did fall!* He thought, as he moved a little faster, turning into the kitchen. And then he saw it. His stomach tightened and he nearly threw up. It felt like he had been hit with a sledgehammer. The blood had run from the bullet hole in her head, forming a perfectly round circle, except on the edge where it had run into the bottom of the board at the base of the cabinets. Estelle was dead.

What the fuck! Marcus thought as his head started spinning out of control. When? Who? Why? The coppery smell of the blood filled his nostrils and he started to hyperventilate, feeling light-headed, until he forced himself to breathe deeply and settle down. Estelle was clearly dead. Checking her pulse and perhaps giving CPR briefly ran through his mind. However, there was nothing he could do for her. There was no type of first aid that was going to help his friend. *Maybe I should call an ambulance?* He thought ... for just the briefest of moments. There was no point in calling an ambulance. She was clearly dead; and he sure as hell was not going to call the police. How would he explain his presence there? *Yes officer, I'm her weed dealer and I just happened to find her here after she sent me a text requesting delivery of two dime bags.* He wasn't a lawyer, but he was pretty sure that wouldn't go over too well.

Think, Marcus. Think. He needed a rag. Didn't have one on him. Backing slowly out of the kitchen, he grabbed the towel hanging on the stove's handle. Coming in, he was certain that he only touched the lamp's switch and the front door's handle after it swung partially open. Retracing his steps exactly, not rushing, he wiped down the lamp's switch as he turned it off. He wanted to leave the room just as he had found it … and without any of his DNA! Backing up toward, and then out the door, he wiped down the handle as he pulled it closed. The screen closed behind him.

Holding on to the towel, he would throw it away in a dumpster on the way home. He thought briefly about calling Train, have him pick him up and get out of here more quickly. No. Bad idea. He had seen enough crime dramas on TV and in the movies to know the police could triangulate time and location of phones based on pings to cellular towers. He didn't want to use his phone anywhere around here. In fact, reaching into his pocket, he turned it off.

Half a block from Estelle's he spotted a dumpster toward the rear of the parking lot of the Golden Dragon Chinese restaurant. Turning into the parking lot his hand encircled the towel in his pocket. As he reached the dumpster he casually, as casually as possible, pulled the towel out and dropped it in. Not more than a quarter-mile later he cursed himself. *What are you doing, Marcus!?* As he started to think more clearly it occurred to him that the police would likely search all the dumpsters in this area.

Doubling back, he took a quick look around as he approached the dumpster. Nothing. It was quiet in the parking lot. Quickly vaulting himself over the front lip of the dumpster he landed with a soft thud. Not much trash inside. He quickly located the towel and stuffed it back into his pocket. Placing his hands on the front edge of the dumpster, he quickly vaulted out.

He was better off taking it with him and burning it. Taking a quick look around, he didn't see anyone or anything out of the ordinary. It was still quiet. Turning toward home, he let his head hang low and he picked up a brisk walking pace. The image of those speed walkers you see at track and field events flashed into his consciousness. Although he felt like breaking into an all-out sprint, and getting away from here as fast as possible, that would have been the wrong move. The absolute wrong move!

If he had looked around more closely as he was leaving Estelle's he likely would have spotted the front hood of a dark sedan - partially lit by a failing street lamp - backed into a nearby alley. Grabbing his phone, Drake sent his text: *to Caine – trap set and sprung.*

[11] FATIGUE

Awakened by the sound of a garbage truck – that was so loud it sounded like it was picking up trash in his living room – making its rounds, Marcus struggled to open his eyes as he climbed out of bed. He was dead tired after a restless night. He had finally fallen asleep what seemed like only 20 minutes ago, before being jolted awake by the truck. Forcing himself up and out of bed, he made his way to the kitchen to get a drink of water.

Glancing at the clock, he saw that it was already 8:22 a.m. He couldn't remember the last time he had slept that late. I guess that was what happened when you have a night like he had and don't set the alarm. Going back to his bedroom, he grabbed his phone and turned it on. It was still off from last night. He was immediately notified of three messages. Two from clients and one from Tracy, about an hour ago.

He would get to the clients later. He was glad to hear from her, which meant she was safe. He tapped Tracy's message: *from Tracy – sorry can't make tonight call ya later.*
"That was probably for the best right now," he mumbled to himself. He needed to figure out this Estelle thing. As much as he wanted to, he couldn't really think about Tracy right now.

What seemed like 1,000,000 thoughts had drifted through his head last night. The one thing he was quite certain of was that Caine was behind Estelle's murder. Now that he knew Tracy was safe, he had to check on his brother. Calling the house, his mother picked up after a few rings. "Hey, Ma. How are you this morning?"
"I'm good, Baby. How are you? I didn't expect to hear from you today, especially this early in the morning."
"I'm good. I meant to ask Marlon something the other night. Is he around?"
"No, Baby. You know he's at school. You missed him by 30 minutes."
"Oh, that's right. I had forgotten what time he left for school. No big deal. Can you please have him give me a call when he comes home?"
"Of course."
"Alright, Ma. Love ya and tell Pops I said hello. Talk to you guys later."
"Alright, Marcus."
It was good to know that Tracy and Marlon were safe.

He knew that Caine had to be behind this. No doubt. However, it was difficult to wrap his mind around the idea that Caine would kill Estelle, or anyone else for that matter, over an imagined transgression. It would appear as if this barbaric act was intended to punish him for continuing to deal weed … and to frame him. How else to explain the text message from Estelle? Clearly she had not sent it. Although he wasn't a CSI, common sense and the drying blood told him that Estelle had been shot before he received the text message and the 15 – 20 minutes it took him to walk to her house.

Ultimately, he knew there were two things he had to do. First, he had to remain calm and think clearly. Fortunately, he had limited his movements in the house last night and he had wiped down the two surfaces he had touched. Unfortunately, there were a number of factors linking him to Estelle and her house: her visits to McDonald's, their exchanges of text messages and the fact that he had been in her home multiple times. And what if someone had seen him, or someone that fit his description, near the house last night?

There was a lot of potential circumstantial evidence. Too much. He had to believe the police investigation would lead them to him at some point. If for no other reason, to see what he might know. While he wasn't a fan of the police, he knew they weren't completely incompetent. The only questions were when would their investigation lead to his doorstep and what should he be doing until then?

He wanted to run all of this past Train. Not only did he trust him completely, it often helped to have someone help you think through a problem, offer a different perspective or consider things you might have overlooked. Grabbing his phone, he tapped Train's picture to send him a text: *to Train - swing by when you have some time to talk*. This had to be face to face. There was no way he was discussing this with anyone other than Train, and it definitely wasn't going to be over the phone, through a text or call. Five minutes later, the reply text: *from Train – taking care of some business this morning be by after lunch*. *Cool*, Marcus thought. *That will give me time to dispose of the towel*.

The second thing he needed to do was find a way to flip the tables on Caine. Along with Drake most likely, they were trying to frame him. Based on all the information he had at this point, they had done a pretty good job, or so it seemed. Now he knew why Drake had followed him, and there were likely occasions where he didn't even realize he was being followed. They had planned this from the beginning. They were looking for a way to get him out of the picture if he didn't go along with what they had in mind. If he didn't join the team and chose to deal weed. He had completely underestimated Caine.

While he waited for Train, he wanted to take the time to get rid of the towel. How to do it? Initially, he had considered burning it. However, the reality was that he could not think of a way to do it discretely. *Going out to the courtyard behind the apartment complex, digging a hole and starting a fire in the middle of the winter was likely to draw some attention*, he thought. Knocking around ideas in his head, he settled on the idea of laundry. Not his own laundry. He didn't want that towel in this apartment any longer than it needed to be. He would take advantage of the laundry room here in the Square.

Gathering his dirty clothes, he stuffed the items in the laundry bag he always used. Going over to his coat, he reached into the pocket for the towel. Nothing. Quickly turning the coat over, he plunged his hand into the other pocket. Nothing. Panic washed over him! What the hell happened to the towel? Did it fall out of his pocket between here and Estelle's? *Think, Marcus. Think*, he told himself. He wiped down the handle on the door after pulling it closed. The screen door closed behind him. Holding the towel in his right hand, he stuffed it in his pocket. He pulled the towel out of his pocket to get to the phone so he could turn it off.

But before he pulled out the phone, he opened his coat and ... grabbing his coat quickly, he reached into the inside pocket, and pulled out the towel. *Oh my, God!* He thought. *After I retrieved it from the dumpster, I opened my coat and stuffed that damn towel in the inside pocket!* He thought he was going to have a heart attack. Just looking at it again, and thinking about Estelle lying there dead, a wave of nausea washed over him. *Get it together! Marcus*, he thought. Taking a deep breath, he tried to relax.

Grabbing his keys, detergent and the laundry bag - with the towel sitting on top - he headed down to the laundry room. If he was lucky, no one would be there, although he figured he could finesse it if someone was, it would be so much easier if the room way empty. Making it to the laundry room, he glanced through the small window in the door. It must be his lucky day. He couldn't see anybody in the room and it sounded like a few machines were humming right along. Perfect. Checking behind him and listening, he determined that no one else was on the way.

Opening the door, he quickly entered. This was definitely his lucky day. There were four washing machines and four dryers in the room. Two washers and one of the dryers were running. Perfect. Looking back through the laundry room door window, he saw that no one was coming. Reaching into his laundry bag, he pulled out the towel. Quickly opening the lid of the first washing machine, he dropped the towel in. Closing the lid just as quickly, he walked over to the last washing machine.

Just as he had finished dumping his clothes in the washer, he heard the door open behind him. Turning, he saw that it was Leanne. He didn't know her that well, but he knew that she stayed on the first floor and lived with her son; Tyrell he believed. "How ya doing, Leanne?" he asked.

"I'm well, and you?"

"I'm tired but I can't complain. Just tryin' to get a load of laundry done this morning before it gets too busy down here."

"I know what you mean," she said, as she opened the lid to the second washer, which had just stopped. Pulling out her clothes, she made her way to an empty dryer. After pouring in the detergent, Marcus closed the door and hit the start button.

"Well that should do it," he said. Not really to Leanne, but kind of to the room in general. "Take care, Leanne. Talk to ya later."

"You do the same, Marcus."

Back in his apartment, he headed straight for the couch and plopped down, before he fell down. His legs felt rubbery, as if he had just finished a half marathon. So far so good. The towel was gone. Whoever owned the clothes in that first washing machine would never even notice a new towel. Who would? It was about as generic a kitchen towel as you could imagine. They would wash, dry and fold it along with everything else as if they had it for years. Wouldn't they?

Going into the kitchen, he grabbed a bowl, some milk and the Lucky Charms. Time to relax with a bowl of cereal with the Irishman. After a second bowl, he got up and turned on the coffee maker and started preparing his mug, adding a little hazelnut creamer and some sugar. The bitter, sweet aroma of the brewing coffee wafted through the air, helping to calm his nerves. Once the coffee was finished brewing, he poured a cup and headed to the living room and turned on the TV. *What were they talking about on Bloomberg TV this morning?* He wondered. Flipping the TV to channel 75, he placed his coffee on the table and took a seat. The host was interviewing the head of a major financial advisory firm:

> Host: "For many Americans, it used to be that your employer provided, and managed, your retirement plan."

> Guest: "That has changed. Now, a lot of the decisions that need to be made with respect to retirement, employees have to make on their own."

Host: "So now the tables have turned. Corporations have stepped back and put the responsibility and much of the cost on the individual. Correct?"

Guest: "Exactly. The pension system has changed quite dramatically. People aren't going to have pensions like they used to, where they get a benefit for the rest of their lives after 20 or 30 years of service. Basically, people are going to retire with 401(k) plans, and maybe an IRA, that they've managed themselves."

Host: "It appears as if the Boomer generation has found itself long on life expectancy and short on income."

Guest: "You're right, Chelsea. I think this is a crisis in the making. Ten or fifteen years from now, people who approach their early 60s are simply not going to have enough money to retire."

Host: "How did we get into this pickle?"

Guest: "It's not something that happened overnight. The story unfolded over a couple of decades."

Wasn't that the truth? "Individuals are pretty much on their own when it comes to retirement planning," Marcus said to the room. After an hour of financial news, Marcus scanned through each of the local channels, looking for any news on Estelle's murder. Nothing. He had no idea how long it might take for her body to be found and reported. He knew it could be today or it could be six months. There were always those stories of bodies found long after they had died.

He had watched *Dreams of a Life* on Netflix not too long ago. The documentary tells the story of a 30-something woman in London whose body was found over two years after she apparently died unnoticed in her apartment surrounded by unopened Christmas presents with her TV still switched on. The tragic part was that she had friends and family; however, through a confluence of different events and factors, no one realized that she had died. For Estelle's sake, he hoped she would be found soon. She was a good woman and he didn't like the thought of her body laying in the house alone, undiscovered.

Just after his lunch of ramen and orange juice, Train sent a text message: *from Train – on the way.* Good. He had been dying to get this story off his chest. He needed to tell someone what happened and to get Train's thoughts on something he may have missed or what he should be doing. While he waited for Train, he ran downstairs and moved his clothes to the dryer. He noticed that the washer that contained the towel had been emptied. It must be in one of the two dryers that was running. So far, so good. He quickly ran back upstairs to be there when his friend arrived. Fifteen minutes later, Train tapped on the door.

"You're not going to believe this," Marcus started. "Remember Estelle? The older white lady with a bad back, really cool."

"Yeah. I met her once. At McDonald's. You told me all about her. Remember?"

"That's right, you did. She's dead."

"What happened!?"

"There is no doubt in my mind that it was Caine behind this. I don't know if he was the one that pulled the trigger, but he definitely was behind it."

"I almost can't believe somebody would kill Estelle, or anyone else for that matter, over this supposed transgression. Apparently it was in retaliation because of the fact that I continued dealing weed. They're trying to frame me. How else to explain the text message from Estelle? There is no way she sent that message." His voice rising and the cadence quickening … "It only took me 15 – 20 minutes to get to her place. She had been dead awhile before that."

"Whoa, slow down," Train said, "You're movin' too fast." Closing his eyes, taking a deep breath and gathering his thoughts, Marcus proceeded to give him the details of last night.

"I had received a text while I was concluding business with Alvin, a new customer. When I left his place, I saw that it was from Estelle, asking for a delivery tonight. You know I normally require six hours notification, but since it was Estelle, I made an exception. I was a little surprised she texted me because I figured it would be another few days before she would contact me for more product. I assumed her back was acting up and she had gone through her supply a little faster to help manage the pain."

"When I got there, I knocked, but there was no answer. Finally, I knocked a little harder and the door swung partially open. I went and looked around briefly. I thought she might be back in the bedroom and I headed that way. But as I got to the kitchen I saw a foot out of the corner of my eye. When I turned the corner completely, I saw her laying there on the floor. Dead. Her head lying in a pool of blood."

"Oh shit!" exclaimed Train. "Get the fuck out of here!"
"Exactly. I had never seen anything like that. I damn near threw up."
"I knew there was no point in calling an ambulance, she was definitely dead. And what if the police had found me there? How would it look if I was there, trying to explain how it came to be that I was in her house, while she was laying in a pool of blood in her kitchen? I knew I had to get out of there! The only things I remember touching were the handle on the front door and the switch on a lamp in the living room. I grabbed a towel from the kitchen, without touching anything, and as I backed out of there, I wiped both off. The lamp switch first, and then closing the front door behind me, the door handle. I left the place just as I had found it. With one less kitchen towel of course.

"What did you do with the towel?"
"I went down to do laundry this morning and I put it in a machine that was already running. I figured whoever that laundry belonged to wouldn't notice one more plain towel in their laundry."
"Sounds like a reasonable assumption to me."
"I was gonna burn it, but I couldn't think of a good way to do it discretely."
"Hmm," said Train.
"What?" said Marcus.
"Nothing. Just trying to think if you may have missed something. Any chance anybody saw you going in or leaving?"
"It's possible, but it was quiet. I didn't see anybody in the area."
"I wonder if that Drake was around, watching? You said you had seen him following you a few times."
"It's possible, but I'm telling ya, I didn't see anything or anybody."
"I hear ya, man. I'm just kinda thinkin' out loud."

"Tell it to me again. From the top. From the moment you got the text message." Marcus proceeded to repeat the story, telling Train everything he could remember. No detail was too small. Everything he could remember, he told to his friend. When he was finished, he asked, "So what do you think?"
"Hmm, it really sounds like you covered your bases well. It was a good idea to jump back into the dumpster and grab the towel. The only thing I can think of is the phone."

"What do you mean the phone? I didn't use it. I thought about calling you, having you come by, pick me up and get me out of there. But I know the police can triangulate time and location of phones based on pings to cellular towers."

"No. Not yours. Estelle's phone. We know she didn't use it to text you. We can assume that Caine - or one of his people, probably Drake - killed her and used her phone to send you the message, luring you to the house. Estelle's phone. Do you recall seeing it in the living room or kitchen?"

"Nope. I don't."

"So where is Estelle's phone?"

They sat there for a minute, lost in silence. Neither said anything. Looking at each other, Marcus said what they both were probably thinking.

"Do you think it's possible they planted the phone here?"

"Considering they shot an old lady in the head, I think anything is possible." Within seconds, they were tearing up the apartment.

There wasn't anywhere within the apartment that they didn't look. Marcus took one half, Train the other. When each was finished with their respective halves, they decided to swap and each would search the other half. Before that though, Marcus ran down to the laundry again, this time to get his clothes out of the dryer.

Walking into the laundry room, he saw that a middle-age woman was folding clothes on the table. While he had seen her around, he didn't know her and had never really spoken to her. He quickly scanned her pile of clothes as he made his way to the dryer containing his clothes. At first glance, nothing. "Hi," he said as he opened the dryer door and started pulling his clothes out.

"Good morning," she replied as she reached down and nudged her pile of clothes to the left, creating a little more room for Marcus' clothes.

"Thanks," he said.

Looking as casual as possible, he started folding his clothes next to his neighbor. Glancing at the stack of folded clothes, he didn't see the towel. Looking at the pile waiting to be folded, he didn't see it. Maybe it wasn't her clothes in the washer in which he dumped the towel? Quickly folding his small pile of clothes, he was finishing up when he saw it. She had reached into the middle of her pile and pulled it out.

And there it was, hanging off the end of her hand, held by her thumb and forefinger. Feeling his heart rate rise, Marcus fought to stay calm. Looking straight ahead, and watching her out of the corner of his eye, he fumbled with his last item of clothing, an old blue t-shirt. She looked briefly at the towel, appeared to consider it for a second, and just like that, she folded it and dropped it on the top of her pile. Relief. Finishing up quickly, he grabbed his stack of clothes and headed for the door. "Take care."

"You too. Enjoy the rest of your day."

Back in the apartment, Marcus passed the good news along to Train. The towel was no longer an issue.

"Perfect," said Train. "That worked out perfect." Resuming their searches, they looked under the couch, under the chair, between the cushions, in every drawer, in the refrigerator, in the medicine cabinet, under the mattress, every cabinet, every nook and every cranny. They looked everywhere! Every conceivable place; and some inconceivable places. After two hours, they determined that the phone was not in the apartment.

"If that phone is in here, the police would never find it. We looked everywhere!" said Marcus.

"Agreed," said Train. "But I've been thinking more about it. If you were trying to frame somebody, would you plant the phone - showing contacts, text history, call history and everything else - in the home of the person you were trying to frame, or would you want the police to find it?"

"Shit! I would want the police to find it."

"Exactly," said Train. "My guess is whoever shot Estelle left the phone there. They would want the police to find it and gather information from it."

"If I would have been thinking clearly, I would have thought about that and looked for the phone."

"Don't be hard on yourself, Marcus. It's easy to think about what you should have done after the fact. Trust me, you did the right things by wiping down the surfaces you touched and getting out of there quickly. Even if you had thought about the phone, you would have put yourself in more danger by spending more time there, rummaging around looking for the thing."

"Whoever killed her probably would not have left it in an openly visible place, knowing that you would be comin' by. More likely, they placed it someplace where it wasn't out in the open, but could easily found by police after a brief search," said Train.

"You're right. At this point, we just need to figure out how to turn the tables on Caine and wait for the body to be found."

[12] THE SETUP

Neither believed that a strong case could be made against Marcus. After all, what would have been his motive? However, they also understood that some uncomfortable facts were likely to come to light with a detailed police investigation, such as the fact that he dealt weed and Estelle smoked it.

Those realities, combined with related circumstantial evidence such as her visits to McDonald's, their exchanges of text messages and the fact that he had been in her home multiple times, could be twisted in any number of ways. It was possible that his prints were on some surface - outside of the lamp switch or the front door handle - within the house. A glass? A coffee mug? *Possible, but unlikely*, Marcus thought. It had been quite a few days since he last visited Estelle and he had no doubt that she had washed any glassware he might have touched in that time.

But what if someone had seen him, or someone that fit his description, near the house last night? All of a sudden his potential involvement seemed a reasonable assumption. Additionally, there may factors they hadn't even considered that could come into play. Were there other measures Caine and Drake had taken to implicate him? The infinite number of possibilities made Marcus' head spin.

Marcus and Train agreed that the only way to minimize the police's interest in him would be to help focus their attention elsewhere. And what better place to focus it than on the person they were certain was responsible for her gruesome death in the first place, Caine. Three hours later, they had talked through numerous options and scenarios, the various pros and cons of each, and eventually settled on a plan to do just that. The first order of business? Identify an abandoned house in the neighborhood. That shouldn't be too difficult. The 2008 financial crisis had ravaged their neighborhood just like a number of neighborhoods throughout Milwaukee, Wisconsin and the country as a whole. Finding an abandoned, foreclosed home would be easy.

Finding the ideal house for the execution of their plan would be the challenge. They needed one that was close to Caine's, but not too close. Perhaps within a two to three block range. And ideally, it would be one that was not well lit by street lamps. They decided they would take Train's car and do a little reconnaissance this afternoon. Driving through the neighborhood, they quickly identified three foreclosed houses that had potential. They would come back tonight to see what the lighting from street lamps was like. This was one of the rare times they were hoping that nearby lamps were broken or otherwise not functional. If they ever needed the Milwaukee Department of Public Works to be derelict in their duties, now was the time.

Since they were out, they decided to hit North 19th Street. While they were familiar with the block on which Caine stayed, they wanted to identify the specific house. That was one of the cards they held up their sleeve. Caine and Drake weren't aware that they knew where their operation was located. Yep, the hunter shall become the hunted. As they turned the corner onto 19th Street, Marcus slouched down into the seat as far as he could, yet still able to see the houses. If Drake, or Caine, were outside by chance, he didn't dare be seen.

While Drake had likely seen Train once or twice, it was unlikely that he was intimately familiar with him and they likely would not recognize his car. "I believe it is up four or five houses on the left," said Marcus. Slowing a little, but not enough to draw attention, Train pulled closer. "That's it," said Marcus as he spotted the sedan and then quickly counted the stairs. Yep, there were nine in all; five in the first set, a short landing, and then four more. The house was right in the area he thought, and there was the sedan out front. They noted the address and made mental notes of the house's description. Picking up the speed a little, they got out of there. Missions accomplished. A few potential abandoned houses to carry out one part of their plan and Caine's drug distribution house identified.

Next, Train needed to touch bases with a few contacts and execute the next two parts of the plan, getting a gun and start planting a bug in the ear of the Neighborhood Watch Leader, Mr. Franklin Pemberton. Back at his apartment, Marcus headed directly to his bedroom. Pulling out the portable safe from under his bed he took out $200. They figured that would be enough for the gun. Going back into the living room, he handed the money to Train. "If that isn't enough just let me know."

"What are you thinking regarding the gun?" Marcus asked.

"Remember Tyrone Jackson from school?"

"Thin, light-skinned brotha with a receding hairline, even back in the 9th grade?"

"Yep, that's him," said Train. "Well, he goes by the street name T-Jax now, and the word on the street is that he deals in some pretty heavy stuff, including guns. I see him every now and then. I don't have his number, but I have a pretty good idea how to reach out to him. In fact, let me see what I can do real quick. Pulling out his phone, he composed a quick text: *to*

Kierron E. – I'm looking to reach out to T-Jax thought you might be able to help.

He followed that with another text: *to Shelly – when did they start distributing drugs from that house on 19th?* Almost immediately, a reply text: *from Shelly – which house?* Train replied: *to Shelly – light gold with maroon trim sometimes a dark sedan out front.* "Who was that to?" Marcus asked. Girl named Shelly. She runs around with Pemberton's niece.

The plan to turn the tables was underway and the first few objectives had been accomplished. However, the first few were easy. They now had to turn their attention to the most difficult task, the one upon which everything else hinged. Fail - and while Marcus might still be able to escape the long arm of the law, and maybe not - Caine would elude the spotlight and he certainly would not be forced to pay for his crime.

It all started with putting Caine on the police's radar. After giving it considerable thought, Marcus and Train only had one idea, and it required Marcus to go back into Estelle's house. And since they didn't know when her body might be discovered, that meant going back in as soon as possible. That meant tonight. They couldn't wait. Marcus had explained to Train that when Drake took him to see Caine, they gave him a piece of paper with Drake's phone number. Although he had started to throw it out, he kept it. He had placed it in the drawer on his nightstand, which is where it was now.

The operation, if you wanted to call it that, was pretty straight forward. It didn't require a team of Navy Seals or Army Green Berets; although if they were available on a per job basis, he would consider paying the likely princely sum. He had absolutely no desire to return to Estelle's house. He had no other choice however. They would go over to the house tonight, sometime between 1:30 – 2:00 a.m., and place the paper in one of Estelle's nightstand drawers. *How appropriate*, Marcus thought. From his nightstand to Estelle's.

One potential bonus? Marcus and Train thought there was a chance her phone would be in the bedroom. If he saw it, he would grab. However, he couldn't afford to spend a lot of time looking for it and of course, the longer he remained in the house, the greater the chance of leaving DNA. The police were bound to find the paper with the phone number and that would establish the connection between Caine and Estelle, through Drake. It was the other parts of their plan that would seal the deal. If things went as the planned, and that was a big if, Caine wouldn't know what had hit him until it was too late.

With the plan in place and every angle they could think of covered, Train got ready to go. "I need to get some rest, Marcus and I know you have a shift at Mickey D's in two hours. What time you get off?"

"I get off at 10:00 p.m. which should give me plenty of time to get home, grab a quick power nap and be rested come 1:30 a.m., when you will be coming by to pick me up."

"Sounds good, my friend."

An hour and fifteen minutes later, Marcus was out the door and on his way to work. The only thing he could think of was tonight. While it was possible that everything would go right, all it would take for his life to be forever changed, was for one thing to go wrong. As he saw it, he didn't really have a choice. Unless he could turn the impending police spotlight on Caine, it was bound to land on him, and there it would likely stay.

Work was a nightmare. Not because there was an inordinate amount of traffic or drama, but because he couldn't concentrate on the things he was supposed to be doing. His mind constantly turned to what he had to do tonight. He didn't feel as though it would be overstating it to say that he was at a critical juncture in his life, at only 20 years of age. If they succeeded tonight, everything opened up before him. All the things he was working toward would have a chance to materialize. Fail and he would just be another young black male trapped in the judicial system; another statistic. While he was still better than most of his fellow crew members, even in this reduced state, Antoine, who was running the store tonight as the shift manager, noticed he wasn't quite on his game.

"What's going on Marcus? Anything I can help with. I noticed you weren't quite yourself tonight."

"I'm good, Antoine. I'm not feeling 100%, a slight headache, and I have some family issues on my mind," Marcus lied.

"It is kinda slow tonight and I have enough people here, so you can clock out early if you like."

"Thanks, Antoine, but I'll be okay. There is only an hour left on my shift anyway."

"Cool," said Antoine. "Just let me know if you need something."

"Thanks, Antoine."

The last part of his shift was uneventful and he actually relaxed a little, resigned to what he must do and confident that things would work out okay. As soon as his shift ended, he grabbed his backpack, put on his coat, his hat, clocked out and headed for the bus stop. "Have a good night,

Marcus," Antoine called out as he hustled out the door.

"Thanks, Antoine, will do. You do the same."

Straight to the bus stop and straight home, Marcus was in his bedroom within 20 minutes. Taking a few minutes to set his alarm for 1:00 a.m., he was asleep by 10:25 p.m. Soon after reaching the REM state he dreamt:

In a dystopian future, in a large American city - Detroit? Chicago? - he's riding the bike, a blue Huffy, his parents gave him for his 9th birthday. Everywhere he looks nature has reclaimed the city. En route to Tracy's house he passes through a tunnel and daylight immediately becomes night. The light affixed to his front handlebars, normally highly dependable, flickers, providing just enough intermittent light to guide his way. Even as he breaks on through to the other side, night remains and he's walking. The pale moon above provides the only light. What happened to the bike? Looking behind him he doesn't see his favorite bike, however, he does notice a shadow, but can't see the body behind the tree that created it. Suddenly a high pitched squeal reaches his ear and the shadow lurches toward him. He's running but he's too slow. "Why are my legs so heavy?" he asks himself. Suddenly he realizes he is on an island as water appears before him. Attempting to take flight to cross the water in front of him and avoid the shadow behind, he struggles to takeoff. Only two steps from the water's edge he is able to launch himself into flight but struggles to maintain altitude. He's falling. Falling ... .

Startled awake by the blare of his alarm clock, he reached out and hit the off button. Between the dream and the alarm clock his heart was racing. Laying there for just a moment, he took a deep breath and tried to calm himself. As is often the case with dreams and their ephemeral nature, the details faded quickly. One big yawn and stretch later, he was on his feet and on his way to the kitchen for some juice. Standing in the kitchen, drinking his juice, he felt good, in spite of the dream. He felt rested and now that the moment was almost upon him, a wave of calm washed over him.

Hearing the familiar sound of his phone vibrating on the nightstand, Marcus headed back to the bedroom. As he suspected, a text message: *from Train – on the way*. No need to reply. Instead, he started to get dressed. Feeling like some kind of urban commando, he grabbed a dark pair of jeans, a black sweater and instead of his familiar Packer's knit cap, a dark blue cap he rarely wore. And finally, he grabbed the paper with Drake's phone number and a penlight, sliding the paper into his front right pocket and the penlight into the left. No sooner had he finished dressing, he heard Train's familiar rap on his front door.

There was very little conversation on the way to Estelle's. They had talked about the specifics multiple times in great detail. They had reached the point where it was simply time to execute. The plan was for Train to drop Marcus off a block short of the house. There was an alley he could take, keeping him off the main street and providing access to the house from the back. Approaching from the back, he would walk around to the front, sticking close to the side of the house, and let himself in the open door.

They had determined that it was smart not to have Train drive around aimlessly, trying to time his return. However, they also didn't want him sitting in the car for too long at any one location. That might be too suspicious to anyone watching. Better to have him spend just a few minutes at any one location. Therefore, after he dropped Marcus, he would head over to the Leprechaun Lounge, between 27th and 28th Streets, and park there for three minutes.

After that, he would head over to Conway's Smokin' Bar & Grill, on West Wells Street, and park for four minutes. Both places were chosen because they are open at that time and there would be multiple cars in the lots. It wouldn't be odd seeing someone parked in the lots. After the four minutes, he would drive back, picking Marcus up in the alley behind Estelle's. Between the two lots and driving time, they pegged the total time at 12 – 13 minutes. If all went perfectly, Marcus would be outside waiting for Train no longer than one minute. Train would drive by, he would jump in and they would be gone. Easy, Breezy, Lemon Squeezy.

Approaching the drop-off point, Train turned the headlights off and the parking lights on. Marcus reached for his knit cap and put it on. "Ready?" Train asked.

"Ready as I'm going to get."

"Remember," Train said, "touch nothing and head straight to the bedroom and place the paper in the nightstand drawer if it has one. If not, set it on top. Without touching or moving anything, scan the room and check the drawers of the nightstands, if they have 'em, for the phone. That's all. You don't have time to look elsewhere, it will take too much time. It's too dangerous."

"Yeah, I got it," said Marcus. And just like that, they were at the point of no return. Hesitating for just a second, Marcus grabbed the door handle and started to get out.

"Forgetting something?" Train asked.

"What? Damn!" Marcus cursed as he reached down and grabbed the latex gloves Train had brought.

"Deep breaths, my man. You're alright," Train said, encouraging him. Putting on the gloves, Marcus opened the door and stepped out into the night. Train pulled away silently and turned on his headlights as he exited the alley. Glancing at his watch and making a mental note of the time, *Twelve minutes*, he thought. Letting his head hang low, he walked purposefully down the back alley toward Estelle's.

Approaching Estelle's back yard, he looked around quickly. Nothing. He stepped into the backyard and headed straight to the left side of the house. Hugging the back wall, he walked quickly toward the front of the house. He was thankful there was a little cloud cover tonight, reducing the moon's light. Glancing at his watch, the elapsed time was three minutes; nine to go. Taking a deep breath, he rounded the corner and quickly approached the front door. Opening the screen door, and grabbing the handle of the front door, he let himself in.

The room looked just like before. The stove provided the only light, giving the appearance of a shadow hanging over the room. Making his way past the kitchen, he forced himself to avert his eyes. Reaching the bedroom, he checked his watch. Two more minutes had elapsed; seven to go. Just as he started to step toward the closest nightstand he heard a noise, voices. He froze. He couldn't make out what they were saying but they were getting closer. Definitely getting closer. A single bead of sweat formed on his forehead. His heart rate started to rise, but he forced himself to take two deep breaths and relax, as much as humanly possible anyway. As the voices grew louder, it became clear that they were young and it sounded as if they may be drunk. He remained still until the voices started to fade again, apparently continuing their walk down the street.

Glancing at this watch again, he saw that he had stood there in silence for one minute. A minute lost; six to go. Moving as quickly as he dared, he reached into his left pocket and pulled out the penlight … and promptly dropped it. "Shit!" he cursed at himself, under his breath. Fortunately it dropped straight down and didn't roll. Kneeling quickly, he found it right next to his left foot.

Picking it up, he turned it on and pulled open the drawer. Scanning the inside of the drawer, he saw no phone, only some paperwork and a checkbook. At least that was good, the phone number on the scrap of paper would be mixed in with other documents. Reaching into his right pocket, he grabbed the paper and tossed it into the drawer, letting it land inside naturally. Closing the drawer, he quickly scanned the top of the nightstand with the penlight to ensure he didn't miss the phone. Nothing.

Making his way to the other side of the bed, he quickly went through the same routine, scanning the drawer and the top of the nightstand for any sign of the phone. Again, nothing. *Damn!* Checking his watch, another two minutes had elapsed; only four to go. He had to get out of here. Taking a moment, he stood perfectly still to think if he had touched anything or in any way left some incriminating piece of evidence. He couldn't think of anything.

Three and a half minutes to go. Walking quickly, but calmly, he made his way out of the bedroom, past the kitchen - without looking at Estelle's body - through the living room and out the front door. As the blood had dried, the coppery smell had faded. Turning to face the door, he grabbed the handle, closing the door gently. Turning back around, he gave a quick 180 degree scan of the area. Nothing. He didn't see or hear anything.

Moving back along the side of the house and toward the alley, he walked at a faster pace than when he had arrived. Train should be here at any moment. Glancing at his watch, he saw that 11 minutes and 45 seconds had elapsed since he got out of the car. Perfect. The timing could not have been any better. He waited just behind Estelle's house, looking down the alley to the right, the direction Train would be coming from.

Thirty seconds later, No Train. He stepped back a little more, fading into the shadow of a tree. Another thirty seconds and still no Train. Although he tried to remain calm, he felt the panic setting in. Where was Train? Had something happened to him? Did he get pulled over? How long should he give it before he got out of here, even if it meant walking?

What seemed like five minutes later, even though it was probably only a minute or so, he saw the headlights turn into the alley. The headlights were switched to the parking lights. Stepping out of the shadows he crossed the alley just in front of Train, jumping into the passenger seat as soon as the car stopped. And just like that, they were on their way home. Like a professional that had done this 100 times before, Train drove calmly. Not too fast, which would draw attention, nor to slow, which would also draw unwanted attention. I guess you could say he was driving like the Goldilocks of getaway drivers … just right.

[13] CRIME SCENE

Estelle's death hit the news two days later. Apparently one of her neighbors had not seen her recently and discovered the body when she knocked on the door to check on her and found that it was open. Marcus could relate. The discovery nearly mirrored his own. The shooting was covered by every local station. The pure brutality of it, a bullet to the head, enraged people.

As per their plan, as soon as the body had been reported as being discovered, Train sent out two more text messages to acquaintances in the neighborhood, referencing the drug house over on 19th Street. It was all sure to get back to Franklin Pemberton. At least they hoped so. They had a lot riding on his network of engaged citizens and ultimately, any weight he might carry with Milwaukee's finest.

Although he knew it would happen sooner or later, and it looked like it had happened sooner, Marcus still felt a sense of shock when he heard Estelle's death being reported on TV. Picking up his phone, he reviewed his latest text: *from Train – text messages sent.* "Good," he half mumbled to himself. The next phase of the plan was taken care of. If they were right, Franklin Pemberton, being the outstanding Neighborhood Watch Leader that he was, would be keeping a close eye on the house on 19th Street, now that he had heard from multiple sources about drug shenanigans goin' on in there. *Known to the authorities in general, Caine, with some assistance from yours truly, would soon be front and center on their radar,* Marcus thought to himself.

Arriving on the scene 30 minutes after the uniformed officers, Maynard and Banks, that responded first to the call, Detective Lieutenant Jesse Velasquez was looking for answers. He was also hoping his partner, Detective Sergeant Pete Hawlsey would get there soon. Hawlsey had a personal matter to take care of earlier and they were supposed to meet here. After entering the house, and taking a brief look around, he viewed the body. *Who the hell shoots an old lady in the head?* he wondered. A real tragedy. He was glad he had got there as quickly as he had.

He had every intention of keeping everyone out of the house until the Crime Scene Technicians had done their thing. The last thing he needed was a bunch of Lookie Lous fuckin' up his crime scene. Back out in the front yard, he summoned officers Maynard and Banks. "Bring me up to speed. What do we have so far?"

Maynard took the lead and briefed Velasquez on what was known at that time. "At 6:25 p.m. we arrived at the residence. We were met by Linda Thomas, the victim's neighbor, who discovered the body. She stated:

> "I hadn't seen Estelle in a couple of days, so I stopped by to check on her. I knocked a couple of times and the door opened slightly. After calling out a couple of times and getting no answer, I walked in. I didn't see anything at first, but when I started to go back toward her bedroom, that's when I saw the body in the kitchen. I went back out to the living room and called 911 from the telephone in the room."

We asked Ms. Thomas if she had touched any other surface besides the front door and phone. She indicated that she may have reached out and touch the kitchen counter when she first saw the body. She then noted that after making the phone call to 911 she exited the residence and waited out front for our arrival. Next, we confirmed the presence of the body, notified dispatch of our finding and secured the crime scene."

"Anything else?"
"The victim has been preliminarily identified as Estelle Anne Reese, a 62 year old Caucasian."
"Good. We'll get that confirmed and see what we can find out as far as family."
"Ms. Thomas indicated that the victim had a daughter, name of Catherine, goes by Cat."
"You haven't spoken to any other neighbors?"
"No, Sir."
"Expand the crime scene to the alley behind the house, to the houses on either side, to the sidewalk up here and canvas the block for potential witnesses."
"Yes, Sir."

As they were talking, the Medical Examiner and the CST team, led by Manny Shaw, an old friend of Jesse's, arrived on the scene.

Manny instructed his people to get some lights on the scene while he spoke to Velasquez.

"Hey, Manny."
"Hey, Jesse. What do we got?"
"Officers Maynard and Banks here were first on the scene. Victim is a 62 year old Caucasian female. The only people that have been in the house at this point, as far as I can tell, are Ms. Thomas – who reported the crime –

the officers here, and myself. Ms. Thomas called in the crime from the phone in the living room. I've expanded the crime scene, now just waiting for you and the Medical Examiner to do your things."

"Sounds good. I'll let you know when we're finished so you can get in there."

"Sounds good, Manny. Thanks."

"Ahh, there he is," Velasquez said to no one in particular as he saw his partner pulling up in his unmarked Dodge Charger. Parking and then making his way over to Velasquez, latte in hand, Hawlsey asked, "What do we have, Jesse?"

"It looks nasty, Pete." I was only in there briefly, so I don't have all the details yet. The Medical Examiner and Manny – and his CST team – are in there now. They'll let us know when they're finished. Jesse proceeded to fill his partner in on what he had so far: the victim, the cause of death, the officers that were first on the scene, Ms. Thomas and the daughter.

"The first thing I want to do is confirm the existence of the daughter, a Catherine, and get her notified; have her confirm the identity once they get the body to the Medical Examiner's office. Then I want to get her over here and walk us through the house, see if anything jumps out at her as being wrong, being out of place."

"Sounds good," said Pete. "I'll head back to the office and see if I can track down the daughter."

After confirming the death, really just a formality, and making a few notes, the Medical Examiner stepped aside and let the CST team get to work. The first thing for Manny was to interview the responding officers in the same way Velasquez did. He wanted to ascertain who had access to the crime scene and ways they may have contaminated the scene.

"D'andre, can you take charge of the team and record the crime scene? I want everything: photographs, sketches, video and notes. I'm going to speak with officers Banks and Maynard."

"Not a problem, Manny. We're on it."

Following his interview with the officers, Manny gathered his team as they finished recording the scene.

"Looks good guys. Any issues recording the scene?"

"None," said D'andre. We got everything. Phil took photographs of the entire area and completed a rough sketch, which he will finalize back at the lab; and Nena videotaped a walk-through of the entire house, which should give us a good continuous narrative. We're ready to collect evidence."

"Sounds good, D'andre. Thanks. Let's conduct our search and lift prints from the usual surfaces. Nena, take the bedrooms. Phil, please get the bathrooms. D'andre, get this living room and I'll take the kitchen. Ana, I want you to take charge of recording notes on any recovered physical evidence. Make sure you get it all: time of discovery, who made the discovery, who handled packaging, everything. You know the drill." Ninety minutes later they were done. "Alright, let's get everything in the van and get it back to the lab," Manny directed.

Velasquez headed over to the van while Manny's team was packing it up. "Anything of significance, Manny? Anything you can pass along right now?"

"A little bit. We found a 9mm caliber spent shell casing in the kitchen. It looks like a single gunshot wound. We determined that the lock on the front door had been manipulated, broken. That's why it swung open when Ms. Thomas knocked with a little bit of force. We got our blood sample and we did lift quite a few prints, as expected."

"Also, we found a cell phone under her right hip once we moved the body. Once we examine it for fluids and get it cleaned up, it's all yours. Of course we won't know more until we get back to the lab. You'll get my report as soon as I'm finished. It looks like the Medical Examiner's office is removing the body now. Should be all yours in a minute."

"Thanks, Manny."

"Oh yeah, one more thing. Might be of interest. We found a small baggie, with what looks like marijuana, on the dresser in the vic's bedroom."

"Jeez, everybody's getting high these days."

"We won't be able to confirm the substance till we get back to the lab but I'm going to go out on a limb and say that it ain't oregano. Of course we'll also check the baggie for prints."

"Thanks again, Manny."

Velasquez had just started to reach for his phone, when it rang. It was Hawlsey. "Perfect timing, partner."

"I found the daughter. Catherine Louise Meyers. Thirty seven years of age, lives in Colorado and should be flying in tomorrow."

"Nice work. Found a little bit here. The Crime Scene Technicians did recover a spent 9mm caliber shell casing and a phone. We'll get the phone once they check it for fluids and get it cleaned up back at the lab. They also found a small baggie of marijuana in the bedroom. Beyond that though, we won't know much more until they get everything back to the lab and do what they do. You want to meet me out here? We'll go through the house tonight? Give it our initial walk through?"

"Sounds good. I'm on the way."

Velasquez figured he'd enjoy a cigarette, or two, out here in the cool air while he waited for his partner. Like a lot of people he had tried to quite too many times to count. He had tried it all: the patches, the gum and that new shit, electronic cigarettes. No luck, he found quitting impossible. Unlike a lot smokers he didn't claim to love smoking. He knew it was a dirty, smelly habit that was damaging his health. As much as he hated to think about it he'd probably die of lung cancer. If it wasn't lung cancer it would probably be something else related to smoking and it would probably be years before he would have died otherwise.

Twelve minutes later, Hawlsey pulled up. "I figured we would go through tonight, take a good look around," suggested Velasquez. "Whatever we find tonight we'll combine with any information we get from Manny's team and any input the daughter can provide. Do we know what time she is supposed to be in tomorrow?"

"Yeah, her flight is supposed to land at General Mitchell at 10:25 a.m. She has reservations at the Courtyard Milwaukee Downtown over on West Michigan."

"Sounds good. Once she gets settled, we'll pick her up, take her by the Medical Examiner's office to confirm identification of the body and then get out here to the house."

"Thanks, guys," Velasquez said as he released Banks and Maynard. "I appreciate it. I think we've got it from here." Entering the house, they took a quick look through each of the rooms. A rather plain home with nondescript furnishings, nothing immediately jumped out to the detectives. Nothing that screamed out, 'This is why I was shot.' On the surface, it didn't look like anything had been disturbed or taken. However, they wouldn't know for sure until they got the final results from the CST team and had her daughter visit the house.

Velasquez walked back to the victim's bedroom, where Hawlsey was. "Nothing in the living room, what about in here?"

"Not a lot. Nothing of interest in the dresser drawers or the closet." Holding up an evidence bag, "However, I did find a scrap of paper with a phone number in the nightstand over there, sitting on a bunch of paperwork. No other numbers though and no address book or anything like that."

"Might be something," Velasquez offered. "Maybe between that number and whatever we get out of the address book from the phone, we can find out who she talked to."

Figuring they had done all they could for now, the detectives called it a night. They would be plenty busy tomorrow, meeting with the victim's daughter and reviewing any results the CST team released. Confirming the back door was locked, they made their way out the front door, which had been repaired by police maintenance personnel after the CST team had finished collecting evidence. A crime scene couldn't be secured if you couldn't lock the front door and the yellow tape probably wasn't enough.

"I think we're good for now," said Velasquez as he locked the door.

"Yep," I do believe so," Hawlsey agreed.

Marcus had been restless all day, a bundle of nerves, since learning that Estelle's body had been discovered. Fortunately, he didn't have to work today. The only thing that prevented him from going absolutely crazy was seeing Tracy. He didn't really have to make a deposit, but it was a good reason to get out of the house and see her. She was glad to see him.

"I was just thinking about you," she said as he made it to the service counter.

"I thought I'd come make a quick deposit and say hi."

"I get my break in about 15 minutes if you want to wait across the street at the coffee shop."

"Absolutely."

Twenty minutes later, on her way out the door, she passed Melanie, one of the bank's officers and a mentor of sorts.

"How are you doing today, Tracy?"

"I'm well and yourself?"

"Good, good. Headed out for a break?"

"Yes, Ma'am. Did you need something?"

"No, no. Go enjoy your break. No hurry. Come see me later this afternoon. I wanted to continue our conversation about continuing education."

"Sounds good. I'll do that."

"Make sure you bundle up, it's cold out there."

"Will do. Thanks."

As she approached his table, Marcus stood and gave her a hug. "Have time for a coffee?" he asked.

"I do. That sounds perfect. Thank you. What about you?"

"My coffee should be on the way," he said as he lifted his hand and indicated to the waitress that she could bring two. Over their cups of coffee they agreed to do something that weekend. Seeing her was definitely what he needed.

Tomorrow would be another story. He was supposed to go in at 9:00 a.m. Maybe it would be for the best; help keep his mind off this Estelle mess. Their plan called for a three day gap between the time the body was discovered and the point at which they carried out the next part of the plan. They figured that would be enough time for Caine to show up on the radar of the homicide detectives conducting the investigation and assumed that they would have found the piece of paper with the phone number, making the Caine-Drake-Estelle connection.

Awake before the alarm clock had a chance to scare him awake, Marcus sat up quickly and swung his feet to the floor. He wasn't scheduled to be at work until 9:00 a.m. which meant that he had time to get in a good run. A run is probably just what he needed. A good run always helped him relax and was a great stress reliever. *Maybe the second best stress reliever*, he thought, which brought a smile to his face. Heading to the kitchen, he grabbed a glass of water and then back to the bedroom to get ready.

He would stretch it out this morning and put in a four-miler. Quickly checking the weather at the noaa.gov website, it looked like it was a little warmer than usual this morning. Not Arizona warm, but warmer. Nice. Dressed, he put on his headphones and out the door he went. The weather was warmer than it had been. Stretching briefly in front of the apartment, he looked up and down the street, debating which way to go. Making up his mind and turning up his music, he took off to the right. Taking off at a faster pace than normal, he felt good. He really needed to burn up some of this anxiety. The first song up in the random rotation, *The Way* by Jill Scott, an oldie but a goodie, would go a long way to helping achieve that.

Making the turn at the two-mile point, he headed for home. His watch indicated he carried a 7:13 pace for the first half. Catching his second wind a little sooner than usual, and feeling good, he picked up the pace. There was no reason he couldn't knock out the second half at a sub 7:00 pace. The last ¼ mile he really let it go. Checking his watch as he passed the apartments, total time on the run was 28:30. Doing the math quickly in his head, he had made his goal, averaging 6:55 over the last two miles. He was definitely feeling it. His lungs were burning but it was a good burn. It felt good to get out and run this morning. A long cool down, maybe a ¼ mile walk, was just what he needed now.

Hawlsey hung up the phone and signaled to Velasquez that he should get ready to go. "I just spoke to Mrs. Meyers and she is ready for us to pick her up."

"Sounds good, Pete. Just give me five minutes." Within 10 minutes they were on their way to the Courtyard Milwaukee Downtown over on West Michigan.

Arriving at the Courtyard, the detectives scanned the lobby. Velasquez spotted a tall brunette, 5' 10" or slightly taller, standing at the coffee bar. With her hair pulled back in a tight bun, her angular jaw line and her serious demeanor, she appeared to be every bit the cat.

Her long, perfectly manicured fingers that gripped her cup completed the look. "Tall brunette at 1 o'clock, sitting at The Bistro bar," Velasquez suggested.

"Nah, the frumpy blonde at 11 o'clock, sitting by the fireplace," Hawlsey countered.

"A small wager, say $1?" Velasquez suggested.

"Sure."

"Mrs. Meyers?" Velasquez inquired as they approached the brunette.

"Yes."

"I'm Detective Velasquez and this is Detective Hawlsey. We're sorry for your loss, Mrs. Meyers."

"Thank you. But please, call me Catherine, or better yet, Cat."

"I know this is difficult for you, but our first stop is going to be the Medical Examiner's office. We need verification of the identity. Do you think you feel up to it?"

"I'm as ready as I'm ever going to get, Detective. Is anyone ever really ready to identify their mother's dead body? Please, let's just get it out of the way."

"After that, we'll head over to your mother's house. We're going to ask you to take a look around and see if anything is out of the ordinary. See if anything is missing."

"Sure. Mind if I bring my cup of tea?"

"That's not a problem," Hawlsey said, "in fact, I'm going to grab a Caramel Macchiato for the road." Moments later they were out the door, in the unmarked car and headed for the Medical Examiner's office.

Arriving at the Medical Examiner's office, Hawlsey verified with the staff that the body was ready for viewing. It was, so they escorted her to the viewing area and the technician on duty pulled the curtain back.

"Can you verify that is your mother, Estelle Anne Reese?" asked Velasquez.

"Yes. Yes it is."

"Thank you," said Velasquez as he nodded to the technician, indicating she could close the curtain. Short and sweet. Within 10 minutes they were on their way to her mother's house.

Back in the car, Velasquez wanted to use the 11 – 13 minutes it would take to get to the house to get some background on her mother. "We found what has been confirmed as marijuana in your mother's bedroom. Did you know she used marijuana? Can you tell me anything about her use? Who she may have bought from?"

"Yes, I was aware that she used the drug. My mother suffered from significant lower back pain; neuropathic pain from a pinched nerve and nociceptive pain due to arthritis. Legal medicinal marijuana was not an option for her, so she turned to getting it the only way she knew how. So yes, I knew about her use; however, she never mentioned a dealer or where she acquired it."

"Any thoughts on who might have done this? Anyone she might have been in conflict with lately?"

"No, she got along well with everyone. She really did. She never mentioned a conflict with anyone in any of our phone conversations. She was a very gentle person."

A few minutes later they pulled up to her mother's home.

"I just want to warn you," said Hawlsey, "the home has not been cleaned. That probably won't happen for another day or two. There is still a lot of blood in the kitchen area."

"Thank you detective. I will be okay though."

Detective Hawlsey opened the door and the three of them entered the crime scene, largely undisturbed since Estelle was killed.

"Please take a look around, Mrs. Me … Catherine. Anything jump out at you as being out of place, changed or missing? Anything? Even if it seems insignificant, please let us know," instructed Velasquez.

Scanning the living room once, and then a second time, she slowly shook her head. "No detective, nothing in this room strikes me as being out of place, changed or missing. It has been a while, about seven months, since I last visited my mother, but everything in here looks very much in place and it does not appear as if anything is missing. Briefly taking a look in the kitchen, where the pool of blood remained, Catherine paused briefly.

"Are you alright … "

"I'm fine, Detective," she said, interrupting Hawlsey.

"Nothing out of place in here."

Emerging from the bathroom and the guest bedroom, she indicated that everything was in place in those rooms. Nothing struck her as wrong, odd or out of place. Moving into the master bedroom, Velasquez and Hawley were losing hope that she would find anything. They were hoping there would be something. Anything. At this point, they didn't have much. No witnesses, no forensic results from the CST team yet, they hadn't had a chance to check out the cell phone yet and they had yet to run down the phone number on the scrap of paper they found in the nightstand.

Standing in the doorway, she glanced around once as she moved further into the room. "Nothing."

"Are you sure?" asked Velasquez. Walking to the side of the bed, she scanned the room again.

"No, everything appears to be in … "Stopping mid-sentence, she stared briefly at the nightstand on the right side of the bed.

"What is it Catherine?"

"I'm not sure. Maybe nothing. Can I touch anything? Can I open the drawers?" she asked, glancing at her mother's dresser.

"Yes," answered Velasquez. Everything in here has already been processed by our CST team." Checking each of the drawers in the dresser and then the nightstands, she was clearly looking for something very specific.

"What is it Catherine?" Velasquez repeated.

"My brother's Saint Joseph Medal."

"Your brother? You have a brother?" asked Hawlsey.

This was the first time Velasquez and Hawlsey had heard about a son.

"Had a brother. I had a brother."

"My brother died seven years ago. He was 25 at the time of his death."

"I'm sorry for your loss. How did he die?"

"Car accident. He was struck by a drunk driver while riding his motorcycle. He used to wear a Saint Joseph medal which was given to him by our mother. As far as I know, that was the only thing my mother kept of his. Since his death, she had kept it on that nightstand, hanging on that lamp."

"Can you describe it?" asked Velasquez.

"Absolutely. It was a beautiful medallion. It was sterling silver with an image of Saint Joseph and a child."

"Was the shape a cross, round, oval … "

"Oval, and the words 'SAINT JOSEPH – PRAY FOR US' were inscribed on the beveled edge. The medallion's chain was also sterling silver."

"I assume you would recognize it if you saw it again?"

"Absolutely."

"Do we know if the CST team picked it up?" Velasquez asked Hawlsey.

"I don't know if it was taken in as evidence. Let me give Manny a call," he said as he excused himself and headed toward the living room.

Moments later, Velasquez and Catherine headed back toward the front room. "Is there anything else that you can think of?"

"No. Sorry I couldn't have been of more help. I just can't imagine why anybody would do this to my mother."

"You did great, Catherine. Trust me. Again, I'm very sorry for your loss." Just then, Hawlsey finished his call.

"Well?" asked Velasquez.

"Nope. They don't have a medallion, Saint Joseph or otherwise."

"Yes, can I speak with Sergeant Jones please?"

"May I ask who's calling?"

"Mr. Frank Pemberton."

"Just one moment please. I'm going to set you on hold momentarily." Two minutes later, Sergeant Jones picked up.

"How are you, Mr. Pemberton?"

"I'm well. Yourself?"

"I'm good. How can I help you?"

"Something new has come to my attention and I wanted you to be aware."

"What do you have?"

"Two or three days ago it came to my attention that some people might be dealing drugs in my neighborhood. A house over on North 19th Street. Been watching since then and it has the hallmark of being involved with drugs; a lot of different traffic at odd hours of the day and night. Plus, one of the mother's in my neighborhood watch group says she has seen at least two known dealers going in and out of there."

"Anything else?"

"I just got a name a little bit ago, that is why I'm calling you now. I figure you could use that Internet or your computer to look 'em up and see if you have anything on him."

"What's the name?"

"Apparently he goes by the name of Caine."

[14] GAME

"One day to go. One day to go," Marcus repeated to Train as they sat in his living room as back to back episodes of the second season of *House of Cards* played, largely ignored, on Netflix in the background. Although they were anxious to get on with it, they had to be patient. The most critical part of their plan required Caine to be firmly on the police's radar. They were only going to get one chance. They had to get it right. While both had to work today, they both had immediately made plans to be off tomorrow once the news of Estelle's death broke.

As episode four ended, Train had to go and Marcus had to get ready for work. They had finalized their plans for tomorrow and agreed that Train would pick Marcus up at 5:00 p.m. Because they didn't know the exact time they would be able to execute the first part of the plan, they weren't sure how long the overall mission would take. It could be anywhere between three and ten hours. In any event, tomorrow was definitely going to be a long day.

"Well, my man," Marcus said, "the time has just about come. I think we're ready."

"No doubt," agreed Train. "We're ready. Tomorrow at 5:00?"

"Yep, tomorrow at 5:00. See ya then."

Velasquez and Hawlsey were finally making some headway. They had learned about the missing medallion. They had the results from the CST team and they had Ms. Reese's phone. In short order, they had identified the five people with whom Estelle had the most phone contact and they would try to reach out to them today, along with the owner of the phone number found on the scrap piece of paper; a Mr. Charles Drake Knowles. Mrs. Meyers was going to be in town for a few more days to take care of funeral arrangements, so she would be available if they had more questions.

For now however, Velasquez and Hawlsey planned to run down the people associated with the phone numbers they had come across. First up was a Mr. Jack Johnson. He turned out to be a former co-worker who stayed in touch with Ms. Reese after her retirement. During their conversations, she never mentioned friction with anyone or potential enemies.

"She really was a gentle soul. I can't imagine why anyone would want to do her harm. Her death is truly a shame." And though they talked on a regular basis and he knew about her lower back pain, he was not aware that she smoked marijuana.

"Well good for her," he said, "I'm glad she found something to help her manage the pain."

Next on their list was a Ms. Mary Shaw, a long-time friend who was devastated by Ms. Reese's death. In fact, she had a difficult time talking coherently to the detectives.

"I'm very sorry for your loss, Ms. Shaw," said Velasquez, in an effort to comfort her. "We're not in a hurry, dear, please take your time." Like Mr. Johnson, she couldn't recall any conversations where Ms. Reese mentioned conflict with anyone. She described Ms. Reese in almost identical terms as Mr. Johnson.

"She was the most thoughtful and gentle person I knew. I can't imagine why anyone would want to do her harm. A travesty. A real travesty," she bemoaned.

The next two interviews with acquaintances were very much the same.

"Apparently she didn't have a beef with anyone and was an incredibly thoughtful person," said Hawlsey.

"Yep, that would appear to be the case," Velasquez agreed.

"Who is last on the list?" Hawlsey asked.

"A Mr. Marcus Williams," Velasquez replied. "I spoke to him earlier as he was on his way to work. He says we can talk to him there."

"Sounds good. Where we headed?"

"The McDonald's over on West Wisconsin. This should be interesting."

"Why's that?" Hawlsey asked.

"Sounded like a young guy on the phone. What kind of relationship would a young 20-something have with a 60-something woman?"

"Are you thinking cougar?" asked Hawlsey.

"No. Get your mind out of the gutter."

"I'm thinking maybe he's her dealer?"

"Could be," agreed Hawlsey.

"I don't know, I guess we'll find out soon enough."

"Yep, we'll see."

Watching their arrival, Marcus felt his heart rate rise a little. However, he felt relatively calm. As calm as could be expected considering the circumstances. He knew this moment would come from the minute this nightmare began. More specifically, he knew the detectives would be coming by here today after he spoke to the lead detective, a Lieutenant Velasquez, earlier today. *Deep breaths*, he thought to himself as the next guest approached the counter.

"Welcome to McDonald's, how may I help you?" Watching out of the corner of his eye as they entered, it appeared as if they were going to speak to Vanessa first.

Arriving at the restaurant, Velasquez and Hawlsey decided to speak with the store manager first, a Ms. Vanessa Steele. A crew member pointed her out and they immediately introduced themselves. She suggested they speak back in her office. Sitting with her in the cramped manager's office, they cut right to the chase.

"We are investigating the murder of a Ms. Estelle Reese," said Velasquez as Hawlsey slid a picture of the deceased across the desk.

"Do you recognize her?"

"No I ... hold on, yes I do. I didn't know her name, but she stopped in occasionally. I wouldn't say she was a regular, but she stopped in often enough that I recognize her."

"Did she have a relationship with Mr. Williams?"

"I'm not sure exactly what you mean by relationship, but they did appear to be friendly. Although Marcus is friendly with all of our guests, particularly those we see on a regular basis, I suppose it's fair to say that he was even more friendly with her."

"How well do you know Mr. Williams?"

"As well as I know any of the crew members I suppose, maybe a little better. I only know him within the context of his employment here. We don't socialize outside of here. However, he has been here over a year and he is one of my better employees. Although a few minutes late on occasion, he is generally on time, works well, doesn't complain, and like I said, friendly with the customers. He's very personable."

"Any indication that he is involved with dealing drugs. Dealing marijuana?" asked Velasquez.

"Excuse me?"

"Do you know if he uses or deals marijuana?"

"Not as far as I know. If I had heard anything along those lines he would have been gone. Obviously that is not acceptable behavior from our employees."

"Do you mind if we speak to him?"

"Of course not. Do you want to do it here?"

"If it's okay with you."

"Sure. I'll go get him."

Approaching the front counter, Vanessa signaled for Amber to take Marcus' place at the register after his current customer. When he was finished, Vanessa approached him.

"A couple of detectives want to speak with you, Marcus, in my office. You can go on back."

"Thanks," he managed. Reaching Vanessa's office he grabbed the door handle, took a final deep breath, and let himself in. Looking at the two detectives sitting there, he assumed the older one was Velasquez, the detective he had spoken to earlier. Standing, the detectives introduced themselves - he was right - and they all sat down. Having mentally run through what he believed were potential questions, Marcus was ready.

Velasquez started the conversation. "Thanks for speaking with us, Marcus. Do you mind if I call you Marcus?"

"Sure, Marcus is fine."

"What was your relationship with Ms. Reese?"

"She was a semi-regular customer … "

"What do you mean by semi-regular?" asked Hawlsey.

"She didn't come by on a regular basis necessarily, but she came in often enough that I got to know her. She liked to come in and get a cup of coffee and sometimes, a sandwich; she liked chicken sandwiches. We became friends over time"

"Was that your only contact with her?" asked Velasquez.

"No. I occasionally went by her house."

"So you've been in her house?"

"Yes, multiple times in fact." A full 30 seconds passed and no one said anything. After seeing that Marcus wasn't going to offer more on his own, Velasquez asked the obvious follow-up question. "What led you to visiting at her home?"

"She suffered from some lower back pain. Arthritis I believe. During one of our early conversations here at the restaurant, she mentioned it. I offered to bring her sandwiches when her back was acting up. Probably once or twice every couple of weeks. Not that often."

"That's a little unusual, isn't it?"

"I guess. But she was nice and we got along well. I liked to talk to her. We talked about going to college and stuff like that, often over a cup of coffee. She always encouraged me to continue my education and work hard."

"Did you talk to her a lot? Did she call you often?"

"Not really. We usually exchanged text messages. She was pretty much up to speed regarding technology even though she was older. She was cool."

Both detectives sensed a touch of sadness as he talked about her.

"You said she mentioned lower back pain."

"Yes."

"Did she ever mention anything about using marijuana?" asked Velasquez.

"Yes, she did."

"She did?"

"Yes. She said it helped with her back."

"Did she ever mention where she got it from?"

"No, I don't believe so."

Velasquez and Hawlsey just sat there, quiet for awhile. Sensing that they were waiting for him to offer more, his heart rate started to rise a little. However, this was all probably part of the game. People often felt the need to fill the void, fill the silence, with noise. Too much silence made them uncomfortable and they started to ramble on to fill that void. He imagined that people probably ended up saying something they would later regret. He wouldn't fall into that trap, if in fact that's what it was. Answer their direct questions. No more, no less. That was the plan. So the three of them just sat there, for what felt like 10 minutes, but was probably not more than 45 seconds or so.

"Well I believe that does it for us, Marcus. Any questions for us?" asked Velasquez.

"No, I don't believe so, Sir."

"Well, thank you for your time. Is it alright if we contact you again if we have more questions."

"Yes. Absolutely. Estelle was very thoughtful. A nice person. Anything I can do to help find her killer." *Hmm, he sounds just like everybody that knew her*, Velasquez thought to himself. Apparently she was a nice person who had no enemies.

"What do you think?" asked Hawlsey when they got back to the car."

"He said a lot of the same things that others said and his boss confirmed they were friendly. There is nothing to suggest that he would harm her. However, the 20-something and 60-something friendship is a little odd. We'll see if he's in the system for anything when we get back."

"What's next?" asked Hawlsey. I'm still trying to track down Mr. Drake Knowles, owner of that number of the scrap paper," said Velasquez. "I haven't been able to reach him. Let's head back to the station and see what we can come up with on Mr. Williams and Mr. Knowles."

"Sounds good."

Later that night, Train dropped by unexpectedly and Marcus gave him a rundown of his encounter with the homicide detectives, Velasquez and

Hawlsey.

"The first thing they wanted to know was the nature of my relationship with Estelle?"

"What did you tell them?"

"That she was a regular customer that liked her coffee. Then they asked about the lower back pain and her use of marijuana."

"And you said?"

"I knew she suffered from some lower back pain and she mentioned that marijuana helped. They asked if she ever mentioned a dealer. I said no."

"Did they ask if you gave her any or sold it to her?"

"Nope."

"No they didn't ask or no you never sold her any?"

"No they never asked if I sold her any."

"I told them that she didn't always feel like going out and that is why I offered to bring her sandwiches when her back was acting up."

"Nice," said Train. "You confirmed that you had a relationship and there is a plausible reason why your DNA might show up in her house if it comes to that."

"They also asked if she called a lot. I said no, but we often exchanged text messages when I would take sandwiches by there."

"That's cool. That explains the contact via text messages."

"Then at the end, they tried to get cute."

"What do you mean?" asked Train.

"The two of 'em just sat there quiet after the last question. I guess they were waiting for me to offer more, maybe say something that contradicted what I might have said before. But like we talked about, I focused on only answering direct questions. No more, no less."

"Sounds like you handled it perfectly."

"We'll see," said Marcus.

"Alright, my man. I'm out. Tomorrow at 5:00."

"Yep, tomorrow at 5:00."

Today was the day. It had been a long few days, but now the time had come to finish this thing. To the best of their ability, Marcus and Train had set the Trap. Tonight they needed to spring it. No work today, which meant he could get a good run in. He wasn't sure what else he would do today, but it was going to be low profile. He wanted to be sure to get some sleep at some point this afternoon and he had to be ready when Train came by at

5:00 p.m.

After grabbing a drink of water in the kitchen, he made his way to the living room where he had more space to stretch out a little. He wanted to get in a real easy, light stretch. He didn't want to stretch too hard. Better to get in a light stretch prior to running and then start the run at a leisurely pace, giving the leg muscles a chance to loosen up. Of course, a cool down and stretch after the run was always a good thing. Slipping on his cold-weather running gear, he slipped out the door and he was on his way. A quarter mile into the run, he realized he had forgot his music. "Damn!" he mumbled under his breath as he warmed a little and picked up the pace.

"Here ya go, Manny," said Velasquez. "One Grande Cinnamon Deuce Latte to brighten your day."

"Thanks, Jesse. But I'm pretty sure it's Cinnamon 'Dulce' Latte."

"Whatever." Getting in around noon, they were getting a late start after working late last night.

"When you gonna finish puberty and drink some real coffee?"

"I don't know, ten, maybe twelve months." This was a running joke between the partners. Hawlsey liked foo-foo coffees from Starbucks while Velasquez preferred coffee, any coffee, that was black and at least moderately warm.

"What do ya got on, Mr. Williams?" asked Velasquez.

"Nothing. He's never been in the system."

"On the other hand, Mr. Drake Kowles … "

"Knowles," Velasquez corrected him.

"Knowles. It appears as if he is, or was, a small time drug dealer. I reached out to our counterparts in Chicago and dug up quite a bit. Not much on Knowles outside of dealing a little bit of weed. However, I found something interesting. Apparently he moved here from Chicago awhile back about the same time as a known big time drug dealer, a Michael Jamal Simms. Known on the streets in Chicago as Caine."

"As in Cain and Able?" Velasquez asked.

"No, as in short for Cocaine. Apparently, that was his product of choice."

"Interesting," Velasquez mused.

"Apparently Knowles and Simms are cousins. So what we do know is that two cousins – one a leader, one a follower – moved here from Chicago a few months ago and at one time, they – or at least Simms – was involved in distributing Cocaine. What we don't know is what brought them to our fair city and what they are doing here now."

"Or their connection to Estelle Anne Reese," Velasquez offered."

"Or their connection to Estelle Anne Reese," Hawlsey parroted.

"Let's gather as much information as we can on these two, including some addresses, and see what we can piece together," instructed Velasquez. "Jeez, all we have at this point is an odd relationship with a young man that works at McDonald's and some unknown connection to former drug dealers from Chicago."

Train arrived just after 5:00 p.m. Marcus was ready, and anxious, to go. However, they wanted to wait until sunset, about another hour, before they left. There was really nothing left to discuss, nothing left to plan. They had discussed what was gonna happen tonight ad nauseam. For the next 50 minutes they sat in relative silence. Each of them lost in their own thoughts, considering the night ahead. At 5:55, Train asked, "Are you ready?"

"Ready as I'm going to get. Let's do this." They made their way to Train's car and soon they would be at their destination. "Got the gun, right?"

"Yeah. I got it. It's in the glove box," said Train."

Sitting down the block, just around the corner from Caine's place, they parked and waited. They assumed Drake was inside since the dark sedan was sitting out front. What they didn't know was how long they would have to wait. This was probably the least known, trickiest part of the plan. An hour later they still waited. An hour after that, they turned the car on briefly to warm it up. Another hour later, still nothing, so they waited. Finally, almost three hours after they first parked, they saw Drake exit the house.

The next part of their plan was pretty straight forward. Follow Drake, kidnap him and hold him at the foreclosed, abandoned house they had selected. It looked like there were some benefits of the housing crisis and financial collapse that decimated Milwaukee and other cities across the country. There were plenty of abandoned houses to choose from.

"Here we go," said Train as pulled away from the curb.

"Yep, let's do this," said Marcus. Slowly they rounded the corner. The hunt was on.

Ten minutes later, Drake pulled into the parking lot of a Bar-B-Q joint not too far from Tracy's bank. Not wanting to be seen pulling into the same parking lot, they continued to drive for half a block, pulling into a parking lot across the street. Because of the distance and lack of good street lighting, it was hard to see exactly what was going on. Five minutes after he parked, a male approached Drake's car and jumped in. He was only in the car for a few minutes and then he was gone. Just like that, Drake's lights came on, he pulled out of the lot and headed in the original direction, driving right past Marcus and Train, who slunk low in their seats as the car passed. Starting the car, Train pulled out quickly and was right back on Drake's trail, hanging back about six or seven car lengths.

Not more than two minutes later, Drake's brake lights flashed and he slowed, his left turn indicator came on and he pulled into the parking lot of a 7-Eleven.

"This might be our chance," Marcus whispered.

"It looks that way," said Train, as it appeared Drake was headed for a parking spot around the side, instead of the front, where there was more light. Slowing down as much as possible, they saw Drake get out and walk toward the front entrance. Pulling into the lot after he turned the corner and reached for the store's front door, they parked two spots over from his car, leaving a space between the two.

Opening the glove box and grabbing the gun, Marcus quickly got out and headed for the back door, driver's side, of Drake's car. If he left the car open, that would make it easier. If not, they would have to confront him as he reached the driver's side door, keeping in mind that he was carrying. Marcus had seen exactly where he kept his gun. Trying the back door, a slight smile came over his face. It was open. He climbed in, gave Train a thumbs up, laid down and waited. Two minutes later, although it seemed like twenty since he couldn't see anything, he heard footsteps approaching the car and the door being opened.

As soon as he heard the door slam shut, Marcus sat up and placed the gun to Drake's right temple.

"Don't even think about reaching toward your waistband. I'll drop you before you get halfway there."

"What the fu ... you don't want to do this," Drake advised. Ignoring him, Marcus pressed on. "Listen closely because I will not repeat myself. Place your right hand on the dash. With your left hand, open the window." As the window opened, Train appeared. "Now, place your left hand on the dash." Drake did as he was told. Slower than Marcus would have liked and reluctantly, but he did it. As soon as his hand reached the dash, Train reached into Drake's waistband and pulled out the gun.

With Drake's gun in hand, he jumped back into his car. The next order of business was to get to the foreclosed home. In Drake's car, Marcus told him, "If you follow my instructions, you'll be fine. If not, you'll die tonight.

Start the car and head over to North 16th Street. Keep it steady and stay within the speed limit. My partner will be following us, and as you know, he has a gun. Your gun." As they got closer to the house, Marcus gave more specific directions. And just like that, four minutes after they left 7-Eleven, they were sitting in front of the abandoned house they had selected. There was a young couple walking down the street, so they sat and waited for a minute, letting the couple clear the area. Meanwhile, Train had parked and Marcus was waiting for him to get into position.

Getting the signal from Train that he was in position, Marcus rolled down his window and gave his next instruction to Drake. Get out and walk toward my partner. Slowly. Don't get cute. These bullets can fly a lot faster than you can run. Opening the door, getting out and walking toward Train, Drake did as he was told. Moving quickly to the back of the house, Marcus maintained his position in front of Drake and Train pulled up the rear. "Open the door, Drake. Don't worry, it's not locked. We made sure of that."

A couple minutes later they were in a back room where Drake was handcuffed to the room's radiator.

"Where's your phone?" Train asked Drake.

"Fuck you," Drake snarled. It was the only response he could manage. Going through his pockets, Train finally found the phone in the inside pocket of his coat. Pulling out a handkerchief, Marcus rolled it and gagged Drake. With his phone and gun in their possession, they were ready to move to the next phase.

"Hell yeah!" Hawlsey said to himself as he finally tracked down the information he had been looking for all day. Something was going on with these characters, Drake and Caine. He had found real estate records at the County Recorder's office that showed Caine purchased two homes at the same time and every indication was that he lived with Drake in one of them. That begged the question, "Why the second house?"

Looking up, he saw his partner walking down the hall. "Jesse!" he yelled out. "I've got information on Drake and Caine." Stepping into the detective's office, Sergeant Robert Jones asked, "What were those names?"

"Drake and Caine. Know 'em?" Just then Velasquez came into the office.

"What are you yelling about?"

"I've got addresses for Drake and Caine."

"Addresses, as in plural?"

"Yep. What do you know, Bob?" Sergeant Jones proceeded to tell them everything his Neighborhood Watch contact had shared about Caine and suspected drug activity at his house.

"I'll be damned. Let's get a search warrant, Pete."

"Yep, and then let's get out of here. It's late and it has been a long day."

Train handed the phone to Marcus while he kept an eye on Drake. Scrolling through the contacts, he found what he was looking for ... Mike. Michael Simms. There it was. In order to execute the next part of the plan required them to get Caine out of the house, out of that back room. The text from Drake's phone should do the trick: *at club textures gonna need backup soon*. Nothing for two minutes. If this didn't get Caine, and Ricky, out of the house, they were sunk. What if it was a different Mike? *Did I just fuck this up?* Marcus thought.

"Anything?" Train asked.

"Nothing yet. Damn!" And then just like that, a reply text: *we're on the way*.

Yes! The last part of the plan was ready to be executed. Checking on Drake, they made sure his gag was tight and everything was out of his reach. Finding an old blanket in another room, Marcus threw it over Drake. "It's likely to get a little cool in here tonight." With Drake's phone and gun in hand they headed out to Train's car. It was a fairly short ride to Caine's house so it would take no time to get there. Even though Caine indicated 'they' - Marcus and Train assumed he was referring to himself and Ricky - they had to be careful approaching the house, just in case they got hung up, and in fact, had not left the house.

Pulling up slowly just down the block from the house they cut the lights, then watched and waited for a few minutes. They weren't sure what Caine - or Ricky drove - so they wanted to be sure they had left, that there was no activity around the house, when they approached. When it was still clear three minutes later, Marcus reached into the glove box and grabbed the screwdriver. It might come in handy. Getting out of the car they closed the doors gently.

Approaching the house, they walked across front lawns, avoiding the sidewalks, which were better illuminated. Reaching the house, they moved quickly toward the back. Train reached for the gate and started to open it slowly. The high pitched squeal immediately cut through the silence. Freezing in place, they waited. And waited. After a minute, not sensing any movement in the house, they slipped through the narrow gap between the gate and the fence post.

Crouching low against the back wall of the house they waited. Listening. Glancing around, they didn't see anything. While Train continued to watch the front sidewalk from the corner of the house, Marcus slowly made his way toward the window to the back room. It was dark and he didn't want to trip over anything. Finally making it to the window, he cursed under his breath as it was higher than he would have thought.

"What?" asked Train, hearing the muffled exclamation.

"The damn window is higher than I thought."

Scanning the backyard he saw a dark object that might be a chair. Walking slowly toward the object, he was pleased to see that it was; in fact, a pair of old chairs. They didn't look too sturdy, but one should work. Grabbing the one that looked the least damaged, he carried it back to the base of the window then motioned Train over and whispered, "It's kind of rickety, hold it for me." Prepared to use the screwdriver if necessary, Marcus tried to slide the window before trying to jimmy it. He thought it may have been locked at first as it didn't budge. With one more effort however, it slid open. Grudgingly, but it opened. Damn thing needed some silicon spray. Opening it just wide enough to lift himself through, with a little push from Train, he brushed against the heavy cloth he had seen from the other side of the room. Just like that he quietly fell to the floor in Caine's back room.

Kneeling and attempting to remain perfectly calm, he listened for a minute or so. Nothing. He couldn't hear any activity out in the kitchen area. There wasn't a lot of light, just the light thrown from the same lamp from the last time he was in this room. Turning back toward the window he whispered to Train, "Hand me the …" Before he could finish, Train shoved Drake's gun through the window.

There was a small desk in the room with a couple of drawers, but Marcus did not want to place the gun in a location where Caine might find it before the police had a reason to search this room. The only other furniture were a bed and the chair Marcus had sat on previously. Walking toward the closet, he hoped there was a good hiding place in there. *Perfect*, he thought as he opened the door and saw various junk on the floor and multiple boxes high on the closet's shelf. Reaching for one that looked large enough to hold the gun, he pulled it down.

Except for some balled up newspaper, it was empty. Grabbing Drake's gun, he wiped it down good. He didn't want to leave his or Train's prints on the probable murder weapon. Placing the gun in the box, he placed it on the shelf, moving it slightly toward the back, and placed a smaller box on top of it. Closing the door, he turned and moved quickly toward the window. He was anxious to be gone. "Shit, slow down Marcus," he said to himself, "I almost forgot."

Going back to the closet, he opened the door and grabbed the box, taking it down off the shelf. Reaching into his pocket his hand found and encircled the Saint Joseph medallion. Pulling it out, he wiped it down lightly and then holding it with the corner of his jacket, he lowered it into the box. Returning the box to the shelf he placed it under the smaller box. After closing the closet door, he made his exit with Train's help. Two minutes later, the window was closed, the chair was back where Marcus found it and they were in the car.

"That should do it," said Marcus.

"Yeah, that should do it," agreed Train.

"Let's get out of here."

Returning to the abandoned house, Marcus and Train were now ready to execute the last part of their plan, getting rid of Drake's car. First however, they needed to check on their guest. Entering through the back door and making their way to the back room, they found Drake just as they had left him. Mumbling through the gag, he tried to communicate. While Train raised the gun level to Drake's head, Marcus stepped to him cautiously and removed the gag.

"I gotta fuckin' pee!" he informed them.

"Not gonna happen, Drake. At least not in the bathroom. It is what it is," Marcus informed him. "Too risky to uncuff you." With the gag returned to his mouth, Drake could only stare with eyes that bore straight through Marcus. No doubt that Drake tried to use his eyes to communicate the level of hate he felt.

Leaving Drake and the house, Train hopped in his car as Marcus hopped in Drake's. The plan was simple as it gets. They would drive the cars East on I-94, take the first exit after the 25 mile point, find a large parking lot - nothing like a Walmart, too many cameras - and abandon Drake's car; wiping it down good before they left. They assumed somebody would report it as being abandoned within a couple of days.

Merging onto the on-ramp to I-94, Marcus started to reach for the volume button on the stereo and then changed his mind, pulling his hand back. He wasn't worried about prints, he was going to wipe off everything he touched once he dropped the car off anyway. Silence. That was what he needed now. Silence and a little time to contemplate what might come next.

The only discernible sound, a little road noise from the car's tires rolling down the interstate, was strangely comforting. The combination of the road noise and the red lights of Train's car in front of him had a strange hypnotic effect. As his mind drifted, he was snapped back to reality as Train's right blinker came on and he veered toward the off-ramp. Glancing at the clock on the stereo, he saw that they had been driving for 30 minutes. It felt like three.

Pulling into the first parking lot, they parked quickly, Marcus wiped down the steering wheel and the door handle as he stepped out. Closing the door behind him he threw the keys in the nearby tree line and quickly jumped in Train's car. Just before dropping Marcus off at the Square, Train let him know that he would reach out to his cousin, Alesia. Have her keep an eye out for any news related to Caine.

"Reaching out to your cousin is a good idea. Maybe she will pass along something that we can use."

"Let's hope," said Train. "Let's hope."

[15] SET

Slowly sipping his Caramel Macchiato, Hawlsey waited for his partner to make it to the office. He had just received the bad news; a small setback. Their request for a warrant to search the home of their new primary suspects, Michael Jamal Simms - aka Caine - and Charles Drake Knowles, had been denied. While the marijuana and phone number found in Ms. Reese's home; and the pair's history of drug distribution were compelling, they weren't compelling enough for Judge Kubrick. They would need more.

Ten minutes later, Velasquez finally showed up.

"So what do you think, Jesse?" Hawlsey asked after he shared the news regarding the search warrant.

"Definitely nothing more than a minor setback my latte drinking friend. Hell, if I was in her shoes, I'm not sure I would have granted the search warrant either. But it certainly didn't hurt to ask. What we need to do is tie ongoing drug distribution to the house. Combine that with everything else and a search warrant is a slam dunk. And based on information provided by Sergeant Jones' informant, that shouldn't be that difficult to do. In the meantime, let's go through everything in the CST team's report one more time. Let's ensure no stone is left unturned."

Where the hell was Drake? Pulling out his phone, Caine looked at the text message for at least the seventh time: *at club textures gonna need backup soon.* Either Drake was never there or no one noticed him when he was there. No one at Textures, a club they occasionally visited, remembered seeing him last night; and certainly no one was aware of any altercations involving Drake.

Caine and Ricky had spent an hour at the club talking to everyone they could and the rest of the night driving around the area, stopping in at places he liked to frequent. Nothing. Absolutely nothing.

"Where is my cousin?" Caine muttered.

"I don't know," offered Ricky.

"It was a rhetorical question, fool."

"A what?"

"Nothing. Just get me back to the house."

Even though it was a late night, Marcus rose long before his alarm was scheduled to sound. This was the best he had felt since Estelle was murdered. He couldn't think of any way last night could have gone any better. The only issue now was Drake. They couldn't leave him at the abandoned house indefinitely and his abandoned car would probably be noticed, and reported, before too long. Moreover, there was no doubt that Caine was out looking for his cousin and the two of them, Marcus and Train, couldn't spend a lot of time over there babysitting him. The detectives would have tied Caine and Drake to Estelle by now and should be working their way to the house on 19th Street. The sooner the better.

Marcus figured they had 24 hours, 36 at the most, to wrap this thing up. Checking his phone, he saw that he had missed a message from Tracy last night: *from Tracy - dinner tomorrow tonight?* It was early, but he wanted to respond right away: *to Tracy - working till 5 but dinner sounds good.* Considering the facts, he didn't have to work until noon and the high stress of the last couple days, he needed a good run this morning. Not necessarily long, but definitely hard.

Slipping into his running gear, and ensuring that he didn't forget his music, he was out the door five minutes later. Going through a light stretch in front of the Square, he soaked in the morning. He loved the relative peace and quiet the morning offered and the easy sound of John Legend that kicked off the random play. Although he normally liked to take off at a nice, leisurely pace, he decided to change it up this morning. A short, intense two-mile run was in order. Finishing up his stretch, he turned to the left and immediately launched himself into a sub-seven minute per mile pace.

Somewhat surprisingly, he settled into the faster pace rather easily. He expected to struggle the first ⅓ mile or so as his body adjusted to the cold weather and he established a comfortable breathing pattern. As the music played in the background of his mind, thoughts of financial security came to the fore. While his parents were by no means destitute, like a lot of people he knew they basically lived month to month, scrambling from paycheck to paycheck. He didn't want that to be him. While he knew a reliable emergency fund, something he had already established, was important, he recently read something on one of the blogs he followed that provided more food for thought.

The idea was pretty simple. In this new economy, young people could not expect to work for one employer for 20 - 30 years and receive a pension when their service concluded. That's not the way it worked anymore. Not only were people changing jobs more often, as more employers abandoned traditional defined benefit plans for defined contribution plans, such as the 401(k), the onus was now on employees to manage their own retirement savings.

Compounding the problem for many Millennials was the fact that there was no guarantee that they would stay in the same line of work throughout their working years. Between the decline of the manufacturing base in the United States and technological advances, many people suddenly found that the need for them, and the job they performed, had disappeared. The answer? Acquire multiple skill sets between education and training; and develop multiple sources of income.

In the post, the blogger made the case that not only should individuals conduct research to find out where the future jobs would be, but should consider the idea of attaining a dual major while in school. An engineering degree was better than a liberal arts degree. Better yet? A dual major such as engineering and business administration; or military service, where someone could learn a skill and earn money for future education. Unfortunately for him, military service was already out.

The same idea was applied to sources of income. The danger of earned income, what some people referred to as labor income, was that you are wholly dependent on an employer for your financial well-being. The way to limit the dependence on one employer was to develop residual, or passive, income. As described in the blog post, passive income is the type of income that continues to be generated after the initial effort has been expended. It is the money someone gets for activities they performed in the past but are no longer required to do for an income. Examples given included the creation and selling of intellectual property such as books or music. *Well, I definitely can't sing*, Marcus thought to himself as he laughed at his inability to carry a tune. "I guess I'll have to think of something else." Multiple skill sets and multiple sources of income. No doubt that there was definitely a lot to think about.

Finishing up the two-mile run at 13:52, Marcus just made his goal. Walking to cool down, he took a few deep breaths to aid in the recovery process. Finishing up his cool down, he walked the short distance back to the Square and bounded up the stairs to his apartment. After a shower and a fresh fruit smoothie, he made his way to the living room, turned on the TV, fired up the Netflix app and melded with the couch for a few hours of mindless entertainment before he had to get ready for work.

After scouring the CST team's report for any clues they may have been overlooked the first four times they read through it, Hawlsey and Velasquez decided their best bet was to watch Caine's house on 19th Street. Heading over to 19th, both knew it was likely to be a long day. If this Caine was any kind of professional, and everything suggested that he was, there would be no obvious indicators of the activities taking place within the house. They would have to be patient and hope that one of his employees or customers fucked up and gave them something to go on.

To say the first three hours were uneventful would be an understatement. Nothing happened. No traffic in or out of the house.

"Don't they make more comfortable sedans," Hawlsey asked?"

"Twenty or twenty five pounds ago you would have probably been a lot more comfortable. I'm going to have to speak to Leslie, find out what she's been feeding you. You're getting a little chunky, partner."

"Look who's talking. You're not exactly a model of fitness, amigo."

"True, but damn I look good!"

"How reliable is Sergeant Jones' informant?" asked Velasquez.

"Jones says he's solid. Takes his neighborhood watch responsibilities seriously. Very seriously." Just then they spotted the first movement of the day. A small SUV pulled up quickly and stopped abruptly in front of the suspect's house. Two males jumped out and headed for the front door.

"What do we have here," Hawlsey mumbled. "Two males approaching the house."

Rifling quickly through their paperwork and pictures, Velasquez pulled out the pictures of Caine and Drake. Holding up the picture of the bigger man between them, Velasquez offered, "Not sure of the smaller man, but the bigger man leading the way has got to be our main man, Caine. Mr. Simms."

"I believe you are correct partner."

"As is so often the case," offered Velasquez.

Approaching the door, the man presumed to be Caine knocked once and the door opened quickly.

"Well, at least we know somebody is in there. Now we just have to figure out what exactly is going on in there and the connection to our victim," Velasquez stated softly.

Twenty minutes later, Caine and Ricky walked out the front door and left as abruptly as they had arrived.

"Do we have anything on his friend," asked Hawlsey.

"Nope, I don't believe so," said Velasquez. Based on the picture we have of Drake, that wasn't him." Jotting down a physical description in his notebook, Velasquez made a mental note to see if they had anything on this potential associate when they got back to the station. The next four hours were pretty similar to the first three. Nothing. "What do you think? Jesse. Call it a day soon and get another team out here?"

"Not a bad idea, Pete. Let's give it another 90 minutes."

"Sounds good." Fifty minutes later they caught a break.

Nodding off slightly, Hawlsey was snapped back to reality when Velasquez uttered his name and nudged his shoulder. "Looks like we have an unknown female approaching the house." Leaning forward to get the best look possible, Hawlsey informed Velasquez, "She looks familiar."

"Oh really?"

"Yeah. Let me think a minute."

"Well, just be ready to give her another look when she walks out."

"I've got it!" Hawlsey blurted out. It's been about four years and I haven't seen her since I was working narcotics, but I believe that's Lindsey. Lindsey Jefferson. Mainly a pill popper, but also liked to smoke weed."

Ten minutes later, she walked out. Again, Hawlsey leaned forward, trying to maximize his view.

"Well what do you think, partner?" asked Velasquez.

"It's her. Definitely her."

"Do you think we have a play here, Pete?"

"I think there is a good chance. My guess is that there is better than a 50/50 chance she's carrying something. No idea if she got it there or not, but she's probably carrying." Approaching her car on the distant corner, they watched her get in and pull away.

"Let's do it," they called out in unison as Hawlsey started the car's engine.

Two miles from Caine's house, they pulled Lindsey over as she made her way down West Michigan Street.

"Hello, Lindsey," said Hawlsey as she rolled her window down.

"I ain't done nothing, man!" she screeched. Tapping on the passenger side window, Velasquez motioned for Lindsey to roll down the window.

"Relax, Lindsey," said Hawlsey. You do realize your right tail light is out and you failed to come to a complete stop when you turned off North 20th?"

"You're kidding me? Hawlser right?"

"Close. Detective Hawlsey. And no, I'm not kidding you. I rarely jest."

"You rarely what?"

"Nothing, Lindsey. You remember me. I'm touched."

From the other side of the car, Velasquez asked, "Do you smell that, Detective Hawlsey?"

"Smells a little like marijuana to me," offered Hawlsey.

"Yep, that's what it smells like to me too."

Turning his attention back to Lindsey, Hawlsey asked, "Got weed in here, Lindsey?"

"C'mon, man. Why you givin' me a hard time?"

"I tell ya what," offered Velasquez. "We can search this car from top to bottom or we can forget about the car and you talk to us at the station about that house you just left over on 19th Street."

"I told you, man, I ain't done nothing and I don't know nothing."

"That's too bad, Lindsey. Make a call, Detective Hawlsey, and get us a tow truck out here. I'm guessing we're going to have to tow this back to the impound lot when we're finished. Please step out of the car, Ms. Jefferson."

"Hold on!" Lindsey protested. "What do you want to know? I can't be sure ..."

"It's cold out here, Lindsey," Velasquez said, interrupting her. "It's pretty simple. Do you want us to go through this car from top to bottom and possibly impound it or do you want to give us an hour of your time, tell us what you know about that house and then be on your way?"

"Alright. I just want this to be over."

"Good. Just pull your car into that lot over there and you can ride with us to the station. We'll get a statement from you and then you can go on about your business."

At the station Lindsey described the house in terms very similar to how Marcus explained it to Train: the reinforced front door, the layout of the house, activities in the kitchen and the back room where Caine stayed.

"So what was your business with this Caine? Why were you there?"

"His partner, Drake, had brought me by there a few days ago. He walked me into the place ..." Sliding the picture of Drake across the table, Hawlsey asked, "Is this the man that took you to see Caine?"

"Yeah. That's him. Goes by the name Drake."

"Continue."

"So anyway, I met this Caine."

"Is this the person Identified as Caine to you," asked Hawlsey as he slid the second picture over.

"Yeah. That's the dude. Basically, he laid out this plan. He was going to run all the drug business in the area. Everything in Avenues West."

"This dude Caine was basically interviewing people, if you want to call it that, to see who he wanted to be on his team as he called it. He said that not all the dealers in the area would have a choice. He would invite some to be on the team, and the rest ... 'Those that were not invited to join the team or chose not to be on the team would be strongly encouraged to cease their operations,' was the way he put it."

"Interesting," mused Velasquez. "Anything else?"

"Nah. I had a couple questions for him but he wasn't there. I talked to some chick named Tanisha for a minute. That's it."

"Who is this Tanisha?" Hawlsey inquired.

"Seemed like she runs things in the kitchen. Was in charge of gettin' stuff ready."

"Is that it?" Velasquez asked.

"Yeah. That's it."

Sliding a notepad toward Lindsey, Velasquez let her know they needed a statement.

"C'mon, man," she protested.

"The sooner it's written up and signed, the sooner we can all get out of here." Forty five minutes later the statement was signed and Hawlsey grabbed his coat.

"You get her back to her car and I'll add this to the other stuff we have and get that search warrant request back in front of Judge Kubrick. If I hustle I should be able to catch her in her chambers. If we're lucky, we'll have it tomorrow morning."

"Sounds good," said Hawlsey.

[16] MATCH

Punching out on the time clock and racing out the front door, Marcus had to get home, get changed and get ready for tonight. Train, who he had texted earlier, picked him up outside.

"What's going on, Marcus? How was work?"

"It was good. No drama. My kind of day. Glad you could meet me here. I figured we talk, figure out what to do next as far as the Drake thing."

"Yeah. That's a good idea. Seeing Tracy tonight, right?"

"Yep. Gotta get home, change and then we're going to meet by her place. It'll be good to see her."

"Seeing Renee tonight?"

"Nah. She's working. Tomorrow night we'll probably do something."

"You checked on Drake earlier, right?" Marcus asked.

"Yeah. About three hours ago. He was mad, but otherwise fine."

"Good. I figure we can't keep him there too much longer; but at the same time, we can't just let him go," Marcus mused. "He knows where I stay and along with Caine, they've already threatened me and Marlon."

"No doubt," Train agreed. "The only thing that is going to force Drake to focus on something other than you will be his need to focus on keeping his ass out of jail."

"Absolutely!"

"Maybe we should check out Caine's place in the morning. Maybe watch it for a bit to see if anything is happening at all. Depending on what we see - or don't see - it might help us make a decision on what to do next with Drake."

"That sounds like the best option at this point," Marcus agreed.

"Well this is you," Train said as they approached the Square.

"Thanks, Train."

"Not a problem. How about 8:00 tomorrow morning I pick you up?"

"That'll work," said Marcus as jumped out and headed upstairs.

"Hold on," yelled out Train as Marcus got halfway up the stairs. Just got a text: *from Alesia - checked database right before I left 2night looks like a search warrant just issued for your boy's house.*

"We definitely need to be there tomorrow morning. It looks like we just may pull this off."

"Absolutely," confirmed Train. "Get a good night sleep, my man. We'll see ya at 8:00."

Arriving back at the house on 19th Street, it was late and Caine was tired. Angry, frustrated and downright tired. Tried to his bones. Summoning Ricky to the back room, Caine laid out his thoughts. "I don't know what the hell happened to my cousin, but something is wrong. Something is definitely wrong. We need to move."

"What do you mean?" asked Ricky.

"I mean we need to get everything out of here and over to the other house. I don't know what's going on with Drake's disappearance and I can't take a chance that it is somehow involved with our operation here. We're moving. Tonight. Get Tanisha and her crew back over here. Now! Start with the shit in the kitchen," he barked at Ricky as he tossed him the keys to his Escalade.

"I'm on it, Caine."

"Damn it!" Caine cursed under his breath, "I don't need this shit right now."

Dinner with Tracy the previous night was great. Both the food and conversation was everything Marcus had hoped for. It was exactly what he needed to focus his attention elsewhere, even if only for a short period of time. This morning however, the focus was back on Drake, Caine and the detectives, Velasquez and Hawlsey. Train would be here in a couple hours and they would check in on the house on 19th Street. Hearing that a search warrant had been issued made the evening even better. This nightmare appeared to be almost over.

Arriving early for work, Velasquez made a beeline for his desk. He was pleased to see the search warrant; approved. While he waited for Hawlsey to show up, he placed a call to Captain Franks, head of the Special Weapons and Tactics division. The indication from Lindsey that the front door was heavily reinforced, combined with the chance they could encounter resistance, heavily armed resistance at that, necessitated the use of the S.W.A.T. boys.

He needed to coordinate with Captain Franks to see what type of support they could get to execute the search warrant. Velasquez was a fan of General Colin Powell and his famous "Powell Doctrine," which advocated for using overwhelming force when facing potential conflict. No need to go in there too light and be unpleasantly surprised.

"Good morning, Sunshine," said Velasquez, holding up the signed search warrant as Hawlsey moseyed in. "We are good to go. I just got off the phone with Captain Franks from the S.W.A.T. division. They're going to support us when we execute this search warrant. Lindsey mentioned the reinforced front door and there is a fair chance there could be some heavy duty weaponry in there. I figured we might as well use the resources at our disposal. Franks said they can be ready to go at 9:30. Will that give you enough time to finish your latte and maybe squeeze in a manicure?"

"Aren't you the funny one? You are in rare form this morning, Jesse. 9:30 sounds good. I'm interested in getting in there and seeing what we can find."

"Well, we know our victim, Estelle Anne Reese used marijuana; we know Caine has his eye on establishing himself as the primary, if not only, drug distributor in the area; and the scrap paper with Drake's phone number establishes the connection between the victim and the would be drug lord. I'm hoping we find something that establishes a forensic connection between the two."

"And a motive," offered Hawlsey. What would possess someone to shoot an old lady in the head? Damn!"

Caine, Ricky, Tanisha and their crew didn't finish until 4:30 in the morning. Taking longer than expected, and getting more anxious, even Caine pitched in, loading shit into the two larger vehicles they had and making four runs, 20 miles roundtrip, between the two houses. He couldn't remember the last time he was that tired, maybe during high school football and two a days?

"Ricky, Tanisha. Get your people out of here for now. We got everything out of the kitchen, which was my main concern. We can get the rest of the shit tonight." He would rather sleep at home in his King size bed but he was too tired to drive. Right now he just wanted to sleep. Soon after kicking off his shoes and laying down on the twin bed in the back room, with his feet dangling off the end, he was out.

"Police. Open up. We have a search warrant!" The sound of banging reverberated throughout the house.

"Police. Open up!"

What the hell? Caine thought. *Where am I? What time is it?* He felt completely discombobulated. Way out of sorts. Slowly it started coming back to him. Late night. Working at the distribution house. Fell asleep in the back room.

"Police. Open up. We have a search warrant!" Just as he started to sit up, the deafening thud from the front room nearly knocked him back onto the bed. Before he could steady himself there were three dudes, S.W.A.T.

stenciled across their bullet proof vests, rifles raised, directing him to get down.

"On your knees, now! On your knees," the first cop yelled. Lowering himself to his knees, the subtlest of smiles spread across his face. *I got rid of all that shit in the kitchen just in time. I knew something was goin' on*, he thought. Caine watched as one of the cops in a suit, a cheap suit, something off the rack from Sears, made his way through the S.W.A.T. team. He assumed it was the motherfucker in charge.

"I'm Detective Velasquez and we have a warrant to search these premises."

"I assumed as much the way ya'll came through the front door. I hope the city is gonna pay to have that fixed."

"Yeah. I'll make sure we get the right forms to you, Mr. Simms."

"Caine. Please. All my friends call my Caine."

"I'm sure they do, Mr. Simms. Take him out to the living room and sit him on the couch. Let's start out there," Velasquez ordered.

Standing out on the porch as the S.W.A.T. team collected their shit and prepared to leave, Velasquez lit a cigarette and asked Hawlsey, "What do you think?"

"I don't know partner. Doesn't look like much in there. In fact, considering the empty boxes in the dining area, I would say this place was recently packed and moved. What do you think?"

"I'm inclined to agree with you. There isn't much in there. This place is practically empty."

"Well, we're here now and we've got the warrant. Let's go through it from left to right, top to bottom and see what we find."

"Yep," agreed Velasquez. "Nothing to do at this point but to do what we came here to do."

Taking the last drag from his cigarette, Velasquez flicked the butt off the side of the porch and stepped back inside with Hawlsey. Back inside they stopped to talk with Caine. "What's going on here, Mr. Simms? Why all the boxes?"

"I was considering moving some things, so I picked up a few boxes. No crime in owing boxes is it?"

"Nope. You are correct. There is no crime in possessing boxes. However, it is a crime to possess, and distribute, heroin, cocaine, weed ..."

"Whoa!" Caine said, "you must have me confused with somebody else."

"Oh really?" Hawlsey asked. "So this is all just a terrible mistake?"

"That about sums it up, detective. You're not going to find any drugs or drug paraphernalia here. I don't know nothing about heroin, cocaine or weed; none of that stuff."

"Interesting. Our sources, multiple sources, tell us something different."

"I don't know what to tell you, detective. Ain't no drugs in here. I can guarantee you that."

"Why the reinforced front door?" asked Velasquez.

"That seems like a lot of door for a house with nothing in it," noted Hawlsey.

"What can I say? This can be a rough neighborhood. I'm just more comfortable with a heavier door. When I start movin' shit in I want to make sure I can keep the riff-raff out."

"Is your cousin around?"

"I got a lot of cousins, man. Which one?"

"That would be Drake. Is he around?" asked Velasquez.

"Ain't seen him for a couple days. Sorry I can't help you, detective."

"I'll bet you're sorry."

With two uniformed officers in tow, Velasquez ordered his team to search the place top to bottom. An hour in and most of the house done, Velasquez and Hawlsey were quickly losing hope. They had gone through the kitchen and the other rooms with a fine toothed comb. Nothing. Absolutely nothing. The only room left was the back room where they had found Caine.

Watching this all play out from down the street, Marcus and Train decided to leave shortly after the S.W.A.T. team called it a morning. There was nothing else they could really see here. Either the detectives would find the incriminating evidence or they wouldn't. Time to return to the abandoned house and release Drake.

Arriving at the foreclosed, abandoned house, they let themselves in through the back door and made their way to the room where Drake was being held. The smell was the first thing that hit them. Like a ton of bricks, it hit them in their nostrils and nearly knocked Train to his knees. Drake had defecated on himself and if Marcus didn't know how ruthless and dangerous he was, he would have felt sorry for him. He looked absolutely pathetic, slumped up against the radiator.

"You might as well kill me!" he seethed through clinched teeth.

"We're not going to kill you, Drake," Marcus assured him. Unlike you and your boy, Caine, we're not murderers. "

"You're going to regret letting me go then. It will be my personal mission to kill both of you."

"Now, now, Drake," Train said, trying to calm him as he raised the gun. "Here is what is going to happen. My boy is gonna step to you and unlock those cuffs. You are going to stay here for five minutes while we leave. And don't try to get cute and leave before then. While I may not kill you, I would have no problem taking out one of your knees. Trust me, let the anger go. You don't want to walk with a limp the rest of your life. It isn't worth it. I believe you will find out soon enough that you and Caine have bigger problems than the two of us. You should have stayed in Chicago, my brotha."

As Marcus approached Drake, Train took a half step closer and aimed squarely at Drake's head. With the handcuffs released, Marcus stepped back.

"Remember," Train said, "five minutes."

Backing slowly out of the room they quickly made their way to the back door and back to Train's car. Glancing back as they pulled away, Marcus did not see Drake. Apparently he had the good sense to stay put for the five minutes.

Working their way to the back bedroom, the last room to be searched, Velasquez and Hawlsey were dejected. What started out as a promising morning had morphed into a wasted afternoon. Nothing. They had found absolutely nothing. Nothing to tie Caine or Drake to drug distribution. Nothing to tie either to their victim. Clearly items had been moved and the house cleaned recently. What prompted the move? When did it happen? No doubt that there was more to this Caine than what met the eye. Unfortunately, it looked as though they were too late to figure out what 'it' was.

Velasquez assumed that whatever was taken from here was either destroyed or moved to the other house Caine had purchased. They could get a search warrant for the second house, but of course, by the time they were able to secure a second search warrant that house would be as empty as this one. "Damn!" exclaimed Velasquez, "This son of a bitch is hiding something. He is absolutely up to no good."

136

"You're right, partner. But let's finish up this last room, make sure we're not missing something and then we'll get back to the station and figure out our next play."

There wasn't much in the room: an oversized chair, a bed, a small desk and whatever might be in the closet. "Check out the desk, Pete, I'll see what we have in the closet."

"Not much here," Hawlsey proclaimed after rummaging through the four drawers rather quickly. "A few documents and office supplies is about it." Pulling items out of the bottom of the closet, Velasquez reported pretty much the same thing.

"Mostly junk on the floor and a few boxes on the shelf. Grabbing the first few smaller boxes, Velasquez opened them only to find air or crumbled up newspaper in most cases. "Mainly a bunch of empty boxes, partner. Truly a wasted day."

Pulling down one of the last two boxes, Velasquez noticed that this was the first one to have any real weight to it. Quickly ripping open the lid, he peered inside.

"What have we here?" he asked rhetorically to himself. Walking over, Hawlsey asked, "What do ya got, partner?"

"Looks like a 9mm, Smith & Wesson, and a Saint Joseph medallion on a silver chain. The medallion is oval shaped and the words 'SAINT JOSEPH – PRAY FOR US' inscribed on the beveled edge. Let's get this gun bagged and to the lab. Call Ms. Meyers and see if she is able to identify this medallion as her mother's. She's still in town, right?"

"I believe so. Not supposed to leave until tomorrow if I'm not mistaken. I'll give her a call," said Hawlsey.

Stumbling out of the back door of the place he had called home for the last two days, Drake made his way to the sidewalk and oriented himself. He was only a few blocks from the house on 19th and he aimed to get there as quickly as possible. He'd have to hoof it since he didn't have his car. Fortunately most people were at work or school at this time of day. However, those that he did pass en route to the house gave him a wide berth. Between the stubble on his face, his disheveled clothing and the smell of feces that hung on him like a cheap trench coat, he imagined he was quite the sight ... and smell.

Being embarrassed, and funky, was the least of his concerns, however. *I have got to get to the house as quickly as possible, find Caine and find out what exactly has been going on the last few days*, he thought to himself. Rounding the corner on to 19th Street he saw two men escorting Caine to the unmarked police car parked in front. Momentarily stunned he just stood there. "Move, Drake before they see you!" he admonished himself. Slinking back around the corner he did an about face and headed back the way he had come. "Nothing I can do for you at this point, Cuz," he said under his breath as he lowered his head and picked up the pace. He wasn't sure where he was going but he had to get away from here.

The text said it all: *from Train - He's been arrested.* This was the first Marcus had heard of the arrest. Later that night he watched the local news broadcast on WISN 12 News. The arrest was the top story:

"Earlier today police announced the arrest of Michael Jamal Simms for the murder of Estelle Anne Reese. He has been charged with 1st degree murder. Ms. Reese was a 62 year old resident of the Avenues West neighborhood here in Milwaukee. She was found five days ago in her apartment, the victim of a single gunshot wound. Prosecutors are requesting that bail be denied."

"A brutal, senseless crime."

"It really was, Craig."

"Thanks, Kathy. The Milwaukee city council ..."

[17] SPRING

Sitting in his apartment with Tracy, Marcus was recounting the dream he had a couple of days ago. "The dream was really vivid. I was flying with ease above the city and enjoying the landscape below. I felt completely liberated. So what's you amateur interpretation, Babe?"

"Amateur?"

"Okay. What's your professional interpretation?"

"That's easy. The ability to fly and control your flight in a dream is representative of your personal sense of power. Flying with ease high above the city suggests that you are on top of a situation; that you have risen above something, that you are in control of something that previously held you back or down. It could also mean that you have gained a new or different perspective on something."

"Well listen to you, Ms. professional dream interpreter."

"That's right and don't you forget it."

"I won't," Marcus assured her as he killed the Netflix app and changed the TV's source input to 'Cable.' Four months after he started, he had finally finished up the second season of *House of Cards*. Now that spring had finally arrived - and the drama of winter with its frigid air and snowy days - seemed like a lifetime ago. He had started the series over and watched it all with Tracy. Although he had gotten halfway through the second season she had only finished the first. "That Frank Underwood is one twisted dude," Marcus said as WISN 12 News at 10:00 p.m. was just starting.

"Absolutely," agreed Tracy.

"Good show. Looking forward to the third season." The 'Breaking News' banner on a bright red background caught his eye. He turned the volume up a little:

> "At the top of the news hour, a Milwaukee man charged with murder was arrested earlier today after evading police for nearly five months. Charles Drake Knowles, 26, was wanted in connection with the murder of Estelle Anne Reese of Milwaukee last October. He was found in a residence in the Near West Side neighborhood of Chicago. His cousin, Michael Jamal Simms, was previously charged with murder and is currently in the Milwaukee County jail awaiting trial."
>
> "Thanks, Craig. Residents of ..."

"I had nearly forgot about that case. They shot that poor old lady, not too far from here. Did they ever find out why?" Tracy asked.

"I don't believe so," said Marcus. "If I remember correctly, they did find the gun, a 9mm, that killed her and a medallion that belonged to her at the drug house over on North 19ᵗʰ Street; and drugs and a lot of drug paraphernalia at a second house they owned. However, I haven't heard anything about a motive. Maybe that will all come out in the trial. But I guess at the end of the day they won't need a motive to convict them. The evidence they have seems pretty damning. I also heard they were able to tie that 9mm gun to a murder in Chicago a couple of years ago. My guess? Ultimately those two are going to do some serious time. Who knows, maybe we'll see 'em on that show you like, *Lock Up.*"

"I'm just glad you got out of that hustle, Mr. Williams. I know you weren't doing things like them, but there are too many crazy people that occupy that world. It's just too dangerous. And it's *Lockdown.*"

"*Lockdown?* I thought it was *Lock Up?*"

"There is a show called *Lock Up.* But I prefer *Lockdown.*"

"Gotcha. I can't keep all your prison shows straight. What's the other one you like? *Overseas Lock Up* or something?"

"No silly. *Locked Up Abroad.*"

"In any case he assured her, they'll be locked away!"

"So true."

"Are you ready to go? I suppose I better get you home. It's getting late."

"Yep, I guess I do need to get home. I do have to work tomorrow."

"Just let me grab my keys."

"Your chariot awaits, my lady" Marcus intoned in his best British accent, which wasn't very good.

"Thank you," replied Tracy in her take on a British accent, which was worse than his. "I know you didn't want to reach into your savings and buy this car, but I'm glad you did."

"Yeah, it hurt to take out that much money at one time, but it was the right move. While taking out the money for the car and 'retiring' from the hustle has left me short of the financial goals I established, it was definitely the right move. There is no way I could get back and forth to two jobs and school if I had to rely solely on public transportation. I should be back on track soon though, now that I picked up the second job at Dollar General. We'll see."

Dropping Tracy at her place, he bid her a good night with a kiss. "See you tomorrow about 5:30 p.m."

"Yep, we've got that economics class. Try not to forget your book this time."

"I won't," replied Marcus. Good night, Tracy."

"Good night, Babe. If you have a lucid dream tonight, make sure I'm in it," she said coyly.

"Alright, Ms. Jackson. Watch yourself now."

Awakened by the lush notes of Smooth Jazz 93.3, Marcus was glad he had finally gotten rid of his old alarm clock. He really had grown tired of being jarred awake. Wiping the sleep from his eyes, he sat up and let his feet fall to the floor. It was going to be a long day. A morning shift at Dollar General, lunch with Train and class tonight with Tracy over at Wisconsin Lutheran College. A busy, busy day. If he hustled he would have just enough time for a quick run and a fruit and vegetable smoothie for breakfast.

Stepping out his front door, the air was cool, but definitely getting warmer for this time of day. Spring was finally here. Thankfully. Taking off at a brisk pace, he settled into a nice rhythm after a few minutes and started to warm up a little. At the 1½ mile point he turned around and headed for home. A quarter mile from the house he ran past Carl.

"Marcus my man, can you square me away today?" Carl called out.

"I told you, Carl, I'm out of that hustle. I've been out of that game for awhile now. Take care." Finishing up strong, he throttled down to a slow shuffle and then a walk. A ¼ mile cool down this morning should work.

Following a quick shower and a smoothie he watered his plants, grabbed his wallet and keys and he was out the door. A minute later the Square was in his rearview mirror and fifteen minutes later he pulled into the parking lot at work.

As a stock person at Dollar General, his job was pretty straight forward. He accepted delivered merchandise, unloaded it, unpacked it, labeled it and stocked shelves. Although the job only paid minimum wage and was neither mentally nor physically challenging, it was a job. That was the most important thing. It served as one element to help him achieve his financial and educational goals. At the end of his shift he punched out and headed to Sal's Pizza where he was meeting Train. A quick text to his friend was in order: *to Train - leaving work see you at Sal's*. Fifteen minutes later he was walking through the front door of their favorite place to grab some Italian.

The smell of fresh baked bread, the hint of roasted garlic and oregano lingering in the air; and the restaurant's warmth were absolutely sublime. Marcus was starving. He grabbed a table and ordered some lemonade while he waited for Train. Two minutes later, his partner walked in. He had recently shaved the chin-fro, Renee insisted, so Marcus was going to have to get used to his new look. It had been awhile since he had seen his friend clean shaven. While they waited for their calzones, the friends got caught up as it had been a few days since they last spoke.

"I assume you saw where Drake was caught in Chicago?"

"Yeah, I saw that," said Train. "I also heard that they tied that same gun to a murder in Chicago a couple of years ago. I would have never thought he could have eluded the police for that long."

"I guess he just kept a low profile, probably had the help of some friends and family in the area."

"Yeah, that would be my guess," agreed Train.

"So how's that new job? Dollar Tree, the Dollar Store?"

"Dollar General. It's alright. I won't be making much money though. Twelve to Fourteen hours a week at minimum don't add up to much. It is what it is though. Been just a little over a week now. Just trying to get used to working the two jobs, juggling the two different schedules. Plus school. It's tough. Seems like I stay tired."

"Although holding the two jobs is tough, it will be worth it. Anything to avoid taking on a lot of debt and I need to stay on top of my financial goals. I have been able to maintain my emergency fund but I'm still working on meeting the goal for my college money. I still have about $12,000 to go."

"Cool," said Train. "I told you I opened a savings account for my emergency fund and I have an appointment with a counselor over at the same school you and Tracy are going to."

"Wisconsin Lutheran College," said Marcus.

"Yep. I'm supposed to meet with her next Tuesday."

"That's good, Train. Real good. How about the IRA?"

"That's next on the list. I only have $300 in the emergency account and I won't be able to contribute much to the IRA but it's a start."

"Absolutely!" offered Marcus. "Like they say, 'The longest journey starts with the first step.' Even if you only manage to contribute $25 a month it gets you into a good habit which will pay dividends later."

"True. So true," agreed Train.

As expected, the calzones were perfect. A little pepperoni, some spicy salami, a little extra mozzarella and a slightly spicy red sauce.

"Man those were good," Train said as he lifted the last morsel to his mouth and pushed the plate away. I think I could eat one of those every day."

"They are tasty. No doubt about that," Marcus agreed.

"How are your folks doing?" Train inquired.

"They're good. Real good. In fact, I was just over there a couple days ago for a little dinner."

"I bet your pops is glad to see you in school."

"No doubt. He's thrilled. I think he appreciates how difficult it is to get ahead without an education. In his day, it was possible. Almost impossible in today's world. While a degree doesn't guarantee anything, it gets you in the game."

"Well, Train, I gotta get going. I'm supposed to pick Tracy up in a couple of hours when she gets off work. We have an economics class tonight and I need to do a little runnin' around first."

"Cool. Not a problem. What are you guys doing this weekend?"

"I don't know. I don't think we have any concrete plans."

"The four of us should get together. Maybe dinner and a movie."

"Yeah, that sounds good," said Marcus. "Tracy was just asking how Renee was doing the other day. Let's plan on it. I'll confirm with Tracy though."

"Sounds good, Marcus. I'll reach out in a couple days to confirm."

"That works." Stepping outside, Marcus started to put on his knit cap, but the cloud cover from earlier was breaking up and it had warmed a little. Stuffing the cap in his pocket, he left his jacket unzipped and took a deep breath. *Nice*, he thought. *It feels good out here.*

Two hours later he sent Tracy a text: *to Tracy - on the way*. She walked out just as he pulled up. "How ya doing, Babe?" he asked as she jumped in and he leaned over to give her a kiss.

"Good. It was a real good day. I had my annual evaluation today and it looks like I'm in line for a $0.25 raise."

"Congratulations! Nicely done."

"You know, we never did finish our conversation from the other day."

"Which conversation was that?" Marcus asked. "We have an awful lot of different conversations."

"That's true," she laughed. "The one where I was asking about you leaving the city, maybe moving out west."

"Ah yes, that conversation."

"Yes, Mr. Williams, that conversation. For real, what are your plans?"

"The truth is, I have been thinking a lot about that. My feelings about the snow and the cold have not changed. I do believe a move to a different climate is in my future ... just not the near future. Although I'm not crazy about either part-time job, they work for now and school is going well. And of course there's a certain young lady I've grown fond of."

"You better be talking about me."

"I might. Spring days like today remind me of why I do like Milwaukee. In fact, I've been thinking we need to make plans to see a Brewer's game. Maybe we'll shoot for something toward the end of April."

"Sounds good to me. I'm not necessarily a big baseball fan, but it would be fun. It's been years since I've been to a game. Live games are so much better than watching on TV."

"Yeah. Maybe the four of us will go. We'll see if we can drag along Train and Renee. In fact, Train suggested the four of us do dinner and a movie this weekend. Do we have any other plans?"

"Nope. Dinner and a movie sound perfect to me. I'm glad you aren't planning to go anywhere, anytime soon."

"Yep, a Brewer's game this spring, spending time at Lake Michigan this summer and then watching the Packers this fall. It all sounds pretty good to me."

WORKS CONSULTED

National Drug Intelligence Center. *Milwaukee High Intensity Drug Trafficking Area Drug Market Analysis*. Department of Justice Archives. April 2007

Wisconsin State Legislature. *Wisconsin Statutes & Annotations, 961.41 Annotations: Uniform Controlled Substances Act*. September 2014

ABOUT THE AUTHOR

James C. Molet is the author of *RENDEZVOUS WITH RETIREMENT: A Guide to Getting Fiscally Fit*. He retired from the United States Army in 2005 following 21 years of service. He holds an MBA from Wayland Baptist University. He lives in Arizona with his wife and can be reached via his website, http://RetirementSavvy.net.